YORK NOTES

General Editors: Professor A.N. Jeffares (*University of Stirling*) & Professor Suheil Bushrui (*American University of Beirut*)

George Bernard Shaw

CAESAR AND CLEOPATRA

Notes by Andrew Parkin
MA (CAMBRIDGE) PH D (BRISTOL)
*Associate Professor of English
University of British Columbia*

LONGMAN
YORK PRESS

YORK PRESS
Immeuble Esseily, Place Riad Solh, Beirut.

LONGMAN GROUP LIMITED
London
*Associated companies, branches and representatives
throughout the world*

© Librairie du Liban 1980

*All rights reserved. No part of this publication may be reproduced,
stored in a retrieval system, or transmitted in any form or by any
means, electronic, mechanical, photocopying, recording, or otherwise,
without the prior permission of the copyright owner.*

First published 1980
ISBN 0 582 78153 1
Printed in Hong Kong by
Sing Cheong Printing Co Ltd

Contents

Part 1: Introduction   *page* 5
   The life of G. B. Shaw   5
   Theatrical background   7
   Relevant ideas   9
   A note on the text   11
   Brief production history   11

Part 2: Summaries   12
   A general summary   12
   Detailed summaries   13

Part 3: Commentary   48
   Nature and purpose of the work   48
   The characters   50
   Structure, theme and style   58

Part 4: Hints for study   62
   Points to select for detailed study   62
   Significant quotations   65
   Arrangement of material   67
   Specimen questions   68
   Specimen answers   69

Part 5: Suggestions for further reading   75

The author of these notes   77

Part 1

Introduction

The life of G. B. Shaw

George Bernard Shaw was born in Dublin, Ireland, on 26 July 1856. Ten years later he was attending Wesley College, a Protestant school, in the mainly Roman Catholic city. He enjoyed reading such works as Daniel Defoe's *Robinson Crusoe,* John Bunyan's *Pilgrim's Progress,* plays by Shakespeare, *The Arabian Nights,* and the Bible. He liked the theatre and was especially fond of opera. This love of music he got from his mother.

In 1872 Mrs Shaw went to live in London with her two daughters, leaving her son in Dublin with her husband. Shaw was by now a clerk in a land agent's business. He was a good worker, but soon became bored with Dublin. London was the centre of British power and culture.

Shaw decided to join his mother and sisters in the Fulham area of London. Through the help of G. J. V. Lee, Mrs Shaw's music teacher and friend, Shaw was able to write music criticism for *The Hornet.* Between 1879 and 1883 he also wrote five unsuccessful novels. In this period Shaw learned to overcome his shyness by public debating; he was inspired to become a socialist by hearing Henry George, the American economist, speak in London; and he was soon to meet Sidney Webb, William Morris and other English socialists. Shaw read a great deal of political theory, including a French translation of Marx's *Das Kapital* (1867). By 1884 he had joined the Fabian Society and five years later edited the famous *Fabian Essays* in which members of the society set forth their socialist theories.

Another influence on Shaw was the Victorian writer, Samuel Butler (1835-1902). Butler's sceptical, satirical intelligence impressed the younger writer, and his ideas on evolution helped Shaw to develop his own theories on creative evolution.

In 1886 Shaw was writing art criticism for *The World.* The music criticism he wrote for *The Star* during the years 1888-90 still reads well. He was learning his craft as a writer. As a critic he was able to study the arts in London. He soon saw that the theatre needed new playwrights who would write intelligently about the urgent social issues of the times. In this, Shaw was influenced by the Norwegian writer, Henrik Ibsen (1828-1906). Like Ibsen, Shaw was fascinated by the new, independent women who rebelled against Victorian ideas of marriage and demanded the right to vote. *The Quintessence of Ibsenism* (1891), based on a lecture Shaw had given the year before to the Fabians, was concerned less with Ibsen's craft as a dramatist than with expounding Ibsen's influential but often misunderstood ideas.

In the 1890s Shaw wrote his early plays *Widowers' Houses* (1892), *Arms and the Man* (1894), *The Man of Destiny* and *The Devil's Disciple* (both 1897), and *You Never Can Tell* (1899). His plays were staged by little experimental societies, the Independent Theatre and, in 1899, The Stage Society. But *The Devil's Disciple,* staged commercially in New York, made £850 in royalties for Shaw. In this same period he became dramatic critic for *The Saturday Review,* writing witty and brilliant reviews which are still worth reading. In 1897 he became a vestryman in the St Pancras district of London, and played a part in local politics. It was during these busy years that Shaw met a wealthy Irish woman whom he married in 1898, Charlotte Payne-Townshend.

In 1903 Shaw resigned from the St Pancras Borough Council. He was defeated in the 1904 London County Council election, but published his ideas on local government in *The Commonsense of Municipal Trading.*

Meanwhile Shaw was writing more plays and getting them staged. The Stage Society produced *Candida* and *Captain Brassbound's Conversion* in 1900 and *Mrs Warren's Profession* in 1902. Then Granville-Barker (1877-1946), the dramatist and man of the theatre, with John Vedrenne (1867-1930), the theatre manager, started producing their celebrated seasons of plays at the Royal Court Theatre. These included Shaw's play set largely in Ireland, *John Bull's Other Island* (1904), *Man and Superman* and *Major Barbara* (both 1905). Shaw also found time to buy his country house at Ayot St Lawrence, battle with another writer, H. G. Wells (1866-1946), in the Fabian Society, write a book, *The Sanity of Art* (1908), and report to the Joint Parliamentary Committee on Censorship. *Caesar and Cleopatra* was produced at the Savoy Theatre by Forbes-Roberton (1853-1937), the leading actor-manager of the time.

Shaw continued to write plays and to join in public debate about the great issues of his day. During World War I he wrote *Commonsense about the War* and even visited the Western Front in 1917.

After the war, many political ideas Shaw supported were in some measure successful. Votes for women were negotiated (from 1918), the Russian Revolution succeeded in establishing a socialist republic, the Irish Free State was set up in 1922 in Southern Ireland, and in 1924 the first British Labour government was formed. Shaw had worked to establish a National Theatre in England, but that dream did not become a reality until after his death.

Shaw had written *Pygmalion* (1914), *Heartbreak House* (1921), *Back to Methuselah* (1921), and *St Joan* (1924), and in 1925 was recognised internationally by the award of the Nobel Prize for Literature. Characteristically, he used the money to aid English translations of Swedish literature, beginning with Strindberg's plays.

His enthusiasm for the Soviet regime led him to visit Moscow and meet Stalin in 1931; he was attacked in the Soviet Press as an outdated conservative. However, Shaw's enthusiasm for this regime persisted. He became dissatisfied with the British system of parliamentary democracy. Meanwhile, in Germany total political power in 1934 was in the grip of Hitler's Nazis. Shaw was by now a famous old man. His best plays had already been written. Sir Barry Jackson had in 1929 established the Shaw Festival each summer in the little town of Malvern. Yet Shaw still wrote plays and political lectures; he also took an interest in the filming of some of his plays, including *Caesar and Cleopatra*.

During the Second World War Shaw's wife died after a painful illness but he lived on to publish *Everybody's Political What's What* (1944), to see the beginning of the atomic age, the post-war Labour government of Clement Atlee, the establishment of a National Health Service in Britain and to be honoured as a Freeman by the City of Dublin and the Borough of St Pancras.

While pruning trees in his garden, Shaw fell and was taken to hospital. He died on 2 November 1950.

Theatrical background

When Shaw first began writing for the English stage, the London theatres were dominated by commercial managements using star actors. In the case of players such as Sir Henry Irving (1838–1905) and Sir Frank Benson (1858–1939) the star was also the manager. They were thus called actor-managers. The actor-manager system had its advantages. It provided a training for young actors who obtained stage experience in small stock parts. Audiences were attracted by a spectacle in which the star dominated everything and everyone by virtuoso acting. Great roles were established, often from unpromising or inferior material, as when Irving played in melodrama. The productions of Irving and Beerbohm Tree (1853–1917) used expensive stage scenery designed to give a realistic, solid, three-dimensional effect. Tree's production of Shakespeare's *A Midsummer Night's Dream* (1900) actually had live rabbits on a carpet of grass in which there were flowers that actors could pluck. Both Irving and Tree sometimes employed an archaeologist to advise them about realistic details in historical stage sets. Irving's productions were also noted for the beauty and care of his stage lighting, as well as for the unity of effect he gained from careful costuming of every character, however minor.

The disadvantages of this kind of production were many. The heavy and elaborate settings required cuts and alterations in the texts of plays, because of the time needed for changing from one scene to another. The stress on realistic illusion was not suitable for all plays. The stress on the star actor emphasised the big scene and the virtuoso role to such an extent that texts were cut simply to draw more attention to the star. Sensational and showy effects all too often occupied talent which could have been working towards a serious art of the theatre.

Shaw condemned Irving's kind of theatre, because he was aware of the new approaches emerging at the end of the nineteenth century. In experimental theatres there appeared ensemble acting in which actors worked as a team under a producer or director. The aim was to offer a serious interpretation of the text as a whole. Shaw's own plays, in fact, were part of this new kind of theatre. In 1904–7, Shaw directed his plays in the Vedrenne-Barker seasons at the Court Theatre. Shaw's early plays required elaborate realistic sets; *Caesar and Cleopatra* demanded settings of which Irving would have been proud. But Shaw broke with the commercial theatre of nineteenth century London by means of outspoken social satire and a stress on the 'play of ideas'; this meant dramatising intellectual debate and the feelings it aroused. The theatre for Shaw, as for other new dramatists in England and Europe, was to be a place of intellectual as well as emotional excitement and energy. This was also true for the non-realistic drama which emerged during the period in France, Germany and Ireland. But Shaw tried to avoid making his characters into mere puppets telling us his ideas. And most of the time he is successful. His plays provide many a good role which nevertheless must be interpreted within the overall effect of the play.

The training of actors in the late nineteenth century was not systematic in England. Amateurs might sometimes join professional companies, and sometimes people with little or no experience would be hired by actor-managers for small parts. Actors might serve a long time in touring companies before making a success. Acting techniques, styles and tricks of the profession could be learned by working in a company, watching other actors and copying them. Star actors excelled in various ways, and their habits became conventions. They took no directions from producers (they were their own producers) nor from authors (they happily adapted, cut and rewrote texts). Shaw deliberately fought this tradition in his long and very clear stage directions. These were written partly because his early plays were published sometimes before they were staged. Full directions were useful to readers and sometimes contained information such as descriptions of streets or a neighbourhood which could not be shown on stage. But these directions were also clear guides to actors and designers as to character, appearance, costume and stage business.

Such was the energy of Shaw's dialogue, the vivacity of his comedy and the effectiveness of his attack on the late Victorian theatre that he became the leading playwright in the English theatre until the 1930s.

Relevant ideas

Shaw had strong opinions on politics, religion and art: in his prefaces and other critical prose he wrote amusingly, lucidly and seriously in order to spread these ideas. He never hesitated to express his views, especially when they were very unpopular, as when he published *Commonsense About the War* during the First World War. This was written not in the excitement of patriotic feeling, but in a practical and very unsentimental manner. He refused to treat the war as an occasion for glory. His attitudes were quite consistent with his earlier, successful plays, *Arms and the Man,* where the main business of the soldier is to scrounge food and keep alive, and *Caesar and Cleopatra,* where the main business of the General is to restore order so that he can collect as much money in taxes as possible. Shaw wrote about his ideas in his prefaces to the plays with joyful, stinging wit. He could see the merits of ideas he disliked or distrusted. This was a great advantage to him as a playwright. It enabled him to give a character very good lines and very strong ideas even though Shaw did not agree with them. He could also see the weaknesses of some of the viewpoints he liked. This meant that a play by Shaw contains conflicts of ideas and characters expressing those ideas which are similar to the conflicts of real life. Seldom are issues very simple and clear. Caesar, for instance, is a good ruler, but he does not succeed in teaching Cleopatra how to be a hero like him. Caesar is kindly and does not hate people in Shaw's play, but we have no evidence to show us that he *loves* anyone. Shaw, of course, deliberately steers us away from the theme of romantic love. Ftatateeta is a bully and a murderer at Cleopatra's command. She is haughty and cruel; but she is also praiseworthy for her courage and her loyalty to Cleopatra. Cleopatra herself is childish, cruel, and vengeful. But Shaw also shows that she has a real desire to learn from Caesar, even if she never fully absorbs his views and methods as a ruler. In his best plays, Shaw is able to make his characters express mixtures of ideas while also impressing us by the energy and life in them as stage people.

Shaw, adapting ideas of the French naturalist and nobleman, the Chevalier de Lamarck (1744–1829), and Samuel Butler (1835–1902), came to believe that a life force was at work in the universe. The life force expressed itself by turning matter into living creatures. Through the evolution of living creatures, the life force tried to become wiser, more intelligent and to gain new powers. According to Shaw, woman's search for and capture of a mate by whom she could bear children was the way the life force worked in human beings. Thus in Shaw's plays women are often stronger than men and more ruthless. They are usually successful because they are in tune with the life force. This theme allied to Shaw's brand of socialism informed *Man and Superman* (1904). In his five plays published as *Back to Methuselah* (1921) it became clear that for Shaw the life force, using matter to express itself, aimed to develop forms which would be able finally to exist without a body.

In this state, the life force would be able to exist for ever. It would be expressed through individual, immortal minds. The expression of the life force in its drive through creative evolution to produce 'supermen' reminds us that Shaw had read Friedrich Nietzsche's (1844–1900) theories of a new morality beyond accepted ideas of good and evil. According to Nietzsche a new kind of man would appear, a superman. Shaw's Caesar is clearly a type of superman. Furthermore, Richard Wagner (1813–83) in his operas was creating supermen out of the heroes of his national myths and legends. He was also striving for a *total art work* in which harmony, instrumentation and poetry were one. Similarly, in *Caesar and Cleopatra*, Shaw strove to express his vision as a unity. His ideas and characters were part of a whole, the total play. The meaning of a play could not be plucked out from the rest of it in the shape of one character telling us the truth as Shaw saw it. The truth dramatised by Shaw was the total play.

Caesar was a hero in Shaw's play, a wise ruler but also one for whom things go wrong. Shaw's comic vision alters the ideas of Nietzsche and Wagner.

During his own long life, Shaw never lost interest in the adventures of ideas. His interests ranged from opposition to vivisection to a fascination with the idea of the saint. His political concerns ranged from Irish nationalism to Soviet Russia. His ideas on diet (Shaw was a vegetarian) even come into *Caesar and Cleopatra*. Caesar's birthday banquet is far too elaborate for the puritan hero. He prefers plain British oysters, though he does sip a little of Cleopatra's wine.

For Shaw, the life of the intellect was crucial, and he was absolutely serious about his pursuit of that life. But his intelligence was a comic one. Fortunately for his readers, his talents made him a major comic writer in his critical prose as well as in his plays. His gifts of clarity, comedy, satire and intellectual energy make him a great teacher. These gifts, together with his craft as a playwright, ensure that even if some of his ideas become dated, his best essays and plays will not.

A note on the text

Caesar and Cleopatra was first published in *Three Plays for Puritans*, Grant Richards, London, 1901. It was revised and reprinted for the Standard Edition of Shaw's works: *Three Plays for Puritans*, Constable, London, 1931. This follows the 1901 edition by including Shaw's preface and notes. The play was also included, but without preface or notes, in *The Complete Plays of Bernard Shaw*, Odhams, London, 1934.

The most readily available recent editions are the *Three Plays for Puritans* (with Shaw's preface and notes), Penguin Books, Harmondsworth, 1946, with numerous reprints, and *Caesar and Cleopatra*, Penguin Books, Harmondsworth, 1951, reprinted 1976. This edition has Shaw's notes, but omits his preface, presumably because it refers to the other plays in the original edition as well as to *Caesar and Cleopatra*.

Brief production history

Fuller details are given in Raymond Mander and Joe Mitchenson, *Theatrical Companion to Shaw*, Rockliff, London, 1955.

30 October 1906 New Amsterdam Theatre, New York: Forbes-Robertson and Shaw give first full professional run in English. The prologue in the courtyard is given, but Act III omitted.

10 May 1951 St James's Theatre, London: famous production with Sir Laurence Olivier and Vivien Leigh. In this production Ra's prologue is cut and the original courtyard prologue becomes Act I Scene 1.

Part 2

Summaries
of CAESAR AND CLEOPATRA

A general summary

Caesar and Cleopatra is set in Egypt in 48BC. Act I opens on the Syrian border near a Sphinx. Egyptian guards raise the alert because Caesar and his Roman legions are close at hand. Cleopatra, sister of Ptolemy, the boy king, is hiding on the Sphinx. A middle-aged man meets her and advises her to show no fear and behave as if she were queen, if she would avoid death at Caesar's hands. She returns to the palace with much more confidence and this makes her act cruelly to her servants. Dressed in royal robes, she manages to greet Caesar who, to her enormous relief, turns out to be the man she met at the Sphinx.

In the palace at Alexandria, Caesar demonstrates his wisdom as a ruler and coolness as a general. In contrast to the inadequacy of Ptolemy, and Cleopatra's adolescent shows of temperament, Caesar gets down to the practicalities of government, arranging to gather tribute money, trying to settle the dispute between Ptolemy and Cleopatra and setting prisoners free. Learning that the Egyptians are attacking, and that the library is on fire, Caesar puts on his armour and takes up a defensive position at the Pharos lighthouse.

Apollodorus comes to the palace with carpets for Cleopatra. She wishes to be with Caesar, who has left orders that she must remain in the palace. Apollodorus smuggles her to the Pharos in a roll of carpet. When the Egyptians attack, Apollodorus and Caesar plunge into the sea and swim for the Roman ships. Rufio flings Cleopatra in after them.

Six months later, Pothinus, still a prisoner, warns Caesar that Cleopatra is treacherous. She orders Ftatateeta to kill Pothinus. His death provokes a riot. Rufio, true to Caesar's law of necessity rather than revenge, kills the dangerous Ftatateeta.

Because of the riots it looks as though Caesar and Cleopatra face defeat and death. Caesar is stoical while the others are alarmed. But Lucius Septimius, who has been fighting against Caesar, wishes to change sides. Caesar accepts his offer, guessing correctly that reinforcements must be very near. Caesar is now able to win the day and leave for Rome, naming Rufio his Roman Governor of Egypt. Preoccupied with business, he almost forgets to bid farewell to Cleopatra, but consoles her by promising to send her a beautiful Roman lover, Mark Antony.

Detailed summaries

Preface to *Three Plays for Puritans (The Devil's Disciple; Caesar and Cleopatra; Captain Brassbound's Conversion)*

Why for Puritans?

Shaw reminds his readers that he worked as a reviewer of London's theatres ('They very nearly killed me'), music, art galleries and recent books. He humorously complains of the effect of all this critical activity on his health. (Shaw's health did, in fact, break down through overwork at this point in his career.) He tells us that *Three Plays for Puritans* was mainly written during his convalescence, and asks himself why the London theatres should have made him so ill.

He now outlines the state of London's commercial theatres at the turn of the century. Shaw says that the majority of the theatre audiences are women who read a good deal and love the unreal world of popular romance. These people like to see good-looking players in fashionable clothes politely making love of a sentimental kind. This would be boring to the wealthy people who can afford to sit in the stalls, but for the fact that such plays really offer beneath the romance a hidden streak of sensuality and lechery. It is, though, impossible to please everyone. Shaw concludes that the playwright should follow the example of preachers and politicians, capturing the audience's attention by using 'some generally momentous subject of thought'. The actor-managers, more successful than other commercial managers, produce plays cut to suit their special talents and made spectacular by lavish sets, Henry Irving being the greatest example of this tendency. Other targets for Shaw's attacks are the musical farces of the day and the 'problem play', merely a feeble imitation of Ibsen's drama. The root of Shaw's objection to such plays is that they pretend to conventional virtues while tickling our vices, supplying shallow entertainment with nothing to enliven the brain or heart, the intelligence or human sympathy. This leads to a demand for seemingly polite plays rather than true drama, which is made from uncomfortable realities. Shaw says that *The Arabian Nights* is a vital treatment of love, whereas the romances of the commercial stage are crippled by hypocritical convention. Art which gives a false picture of humanity is bad and dangerous, because we tend to base our views of human nature, beauty and reality upon the images of these things which occur in art. When romantic sensuousness in art is worshipped above reality, then Shaw's puritanism leads him to condemn such art just as seventeenth century puritans condemned the English theatre of their day.

On diabolonian ethics

Shaw now defends his writing of prefaces by saying that he wishes his readers to be undeceived and have the truth as he sees it. He also likes to explain the merits of his work to that majority of people incapable of knowing good from bad work. His novelty is in his self-advertisement and conceit, yet people think it is his ideas and stage incidents that are new. *The Devil's Disciple* is full of the well-worn devices of old-fashioned playwrights. Its 'novelty' is merely in its advanced ideas which include its diabolonian hero, Dick Dudgeon. To be a diabolonian is to take pity on the devil and defend his rebellion against God—a persistent theme in serious literature. Because the newspaper critics failed to understand this, they failed to understand the play.

Better than Shakespear?

Shaw attacks Shakespeare for using in *Antony and Cleopatra* (1606-7) all his skill 'to persuade foolish spectators that the world was well lost' by lovers. For Shaw, a love affair is not so important. He condemns Shakespeare and Thackeray for their conventional morality which tries to evade despair, and asserts that 'sexual infatuation' is a comic, not a tragic theme. Shaw offers his Caesar as better than Shakespeare's. He then attacks the stunted performances of Shakespeare, fashionable at the time, and the uncritical praise of Shakespeare known as 'bardolatry'. Shaw goes on to say that it is perfectly possible to criticise Shakespeare without being able to match him as a playwright. The writing of plays which work well on stage is not an extremely difficult craft. But a new drama demands new ideas, and the old techniques presented in the light of a new philosophy. Shakespeare, Michelangelo and Raphael, for example, saw things differently from the artists of previous generations. In turn, their view of things was replaced by the different vision of 'a new race of nineteenth century poets and critics, from Byron to William Morris' who rediscovered in medieval art, from the period before Raphael, new features to cultivate. Technical skill alone is not the secret of greatness in art: 'new ideas make their technique as water makes its channel.'

The nineteenth century German historian Mommsen gives a very different picture of Julius Caesar from that of Shakespeare. Shaw replaces Shakespeare's knightly ideal in Caesar with a Mommsenite realistic statesman.

Shaw concludes by reminding us that his dramatic technique is conventional. His reputation for originality is based on the fact that he uses the most progressive thinkers. He hopes that someday the majority will themselves quickly accept progressive ideas, for the fame of writers would then flourish not for centuries, but more beautifully, though only for a year.

NOTES AND GLOSSARY:

Puritans: originally a group of English Protestants in the sixteenth and seventeenth centuries. They wished to simplify religious ceremony and live a sober life devoted to God and duty. The word is now loosely applied to those who feel guilty about pleasure, thinking it sinful, and who follow stern moral principles

Plays, Pleasant and Unpleasant: *Plays Unpleasant* (1898) was a collection of Shaw's *Widowers' Houses, The Philanderer* and *Mrs Warren's Profession. Plays Pleasant* (1898) contained *Arms and the Man, Candida, The Man of Destiny* and *You Never Can Tell*. The preface to this collection of plays is a valuable statement of Shaw's ideas about drama and theatre

Cockney cab horse: a cockney is a Londoner born within the sound of Bow Bells. Many cab drivers are referred to as cockneys. In the 1890s and until motor cars were used, the London cabs were small carriages pulled by horses

not eaten meat for twenty years: Shaw was a vegetarian

drab: a loose woman. To drab is to go after loose women. Later on Shaw uses the word in its other sense of dreary, dingy or dull when he refers to 'drab houses'

stalls: expensive theatre seats on the ground floor of the auditorium. 'The stalls' is also used to refer to wealthy theatre-goers who always buy tickets for these seats

box office: the place in the theatre where tickets are bought. The term is also used to refer to the financial aspect of plays and the theatre

Browning Society: a group devoted to studying the life and works of the English poet, Robert Browning (1812–89)

Shelley Society: similarly, a group devoted to studying the life and works of the English poet, Percy Bysshe Shelley (1792–1822)

Strafford: Thomas Wentworth, First Earl of Strafford (1593–1641), and principal Minister of King Charles I, was executed for treason. He is the hero of Browning's play *Strafford* (1837)

***Colombe's Birthday*:** a play (1853) by Robert Browning. It was not successful in the theatre

***The Cenci*:** a verse tragedy (1818) by Shelley, first performed in London in 1886

Independent Theatre: founded by the Dutchman J. T. Grein in London in 1891, this theatre was influenced by André Antoine's Théâtre Libre (Free Theatre) founded in Paris in 1887 to produce new, experimental and naturalistic plays. Shaw's *Widowers' Houses* (1892) was first staged by the Independent Theatre

Stage Society: founded in London in 1899 for private performances on Sundays of serious new drama, including Shaw's plays. Its activities came to an end in 1939

Ibsen, Henrik: Norwegian dramatist (1828–1906) famous for his poetic and realistic plays which largely inspired a new dramatic movement in Europe and influenced Shaw in particular. Shaw wrote about Ibsen's plays in *The Quintessence of Ibsenism* (1891)

Maeterlinck, Maurice: Belgian poet and dramatist (1862–1949) who enjoyed great fame in the 1890s and early twentieth century. His characteristic plays were part of the symbolist movement in drama

actor-managers: star actors who also managed their own companies of players, both in London and on tour in the provinces

Shakespear: notice Shaw's preference for this spelling of the name of the greatest English dramatist, William Shakespeare (1564–1616). Shaw also preferred the old-fashioned spelling 'shew' for the verb 'show'

Sir Henry Irving: (1838–1905) most famous of the actor-managers, and the first actor ever to be knighted for his services (in 1895). His theatre was the Lyceum in London

Ellen Terry: a famous actress (1847–1928) who joined Irving as his leading lady in 1878, and a friend of Shaw

stock company: a group of actors used for minor and supporting roles in plays produced by actor-managers

Abbots of Misrule: also Lords of Misrule. A title given at one time to persons chosen to lead Christmas games and festivities in a great house

Stage pictures: the visual effects gained from the grouping, posing, gestures, and costuming of actors within the setting created by lighting effects, scenery and stage properties or furniture

pit: cheap seating area in the theatres at the turn of the century. The pit contained hard, uncomfortable seating. It can also mean the people who buy such seats

Macbeth:	Shakespeare's tragedy believed to be written in 1605–6
Justice Shallow:	comic character in Shakespeare's *Henry IV* (Part 2) and *The Merry Wives of Windsor*
bona roba:	*(Latin)* good dress. Used to mean a showy harlot
farthing:	a British copper coin, now obsolete, worth one quarter of the old penny and therefore practically valueless
Lyceum Shakespear:	the kind of productions of Shakespeare's plays presented by Sir Henry Irving at the Lyceum
Pharisaical:	hypocritically self-righteous. The Pharisees of the New Testament were shown to be eager to condemn people's actions by insisting on petty points of law instead of acting according to the spirit of the law
humors:	moods or states of mind. Before the days of modern medicine, it was believed that our temperament was caused by the mixture in the body of four fluids called humours
The Rogue's Comedy:	a play (1896) by H. A. Jones, (1851–1929), the most popular dramatist of the 1890s
The Rake's Progress:	a series of moral pictures by William Hogarth (1697–1764) attacking social evils in eighteenth century England
The Sign of the Cross:	a play (1895) by Wilson Barrett (1848–1904)
Falstaff, Sir John:	Shakespeare's famous comic character, the fat knight of *Henry IV* (Parts 1 and 2) and *The Merry Wives of Windsor*
Doll Tearsheet:	a harlot in *Henry IV* (Part 2)
Romeo and Juliet:	Shakespeare's famous tragedy of young lovers written 1595–6
the conversation of the husband of Juliet's nurse:	Shaw refers to the nurse's comic speech containing her husband's bawdy joke (*Romeo and Juliet*, I.3. lines 41–3)
a poor girl of the pavement:	one of the streetwalkers who would sell themselves as prostitutes
Pasha:	a title used at one time by Turkish military and civil officials
Mrs Warren's:	Shaw is referring to a character in his play *Mrs Warren's Profession* (1902)
the music hall:	a form of theatrical entertainment made up of song and dance acts, comedians, farcical sketches and other variety acts such as jugglers, conjurors, and acrobats. Music hall flourished in the nineteenth and early twentieth centuries

Bohemianism: the unconventional and usually artistic way of life of those who disregard the normal manners and morals of society

Robertson, T. W.: English dramatist (1829-71) who favoured stage realism and whose most famous play was *Caste* (1867)

first actor was knighted in the nineties: see note on Sir Henry Irving on page 16

pounds: prior to the new English decimal currency, there were twenty shillings to the pound. At the time Shaw was writing thirty shillings a week was a modest wage

the manner of the public school and university: public schools in England are, in fact, private rather than state governed schools, and provide education and lodging to fee-paying pupils, usually from genteel and wealthy families. The young people attending such schools and thereafter the university, Shaw implies, did not always have the good manners people expected them to have

Hedda Gabler: the suicidal heroine of Ibsen's *Hedda Gabler* (1891)

***ménage à trois*:** French phrase used to describe a relationship in which a husband or wife takes in a mistress or lover

Judge Brack: in Ibsen's *Hedda Gabler*, Brack, a friend of Hedda and her husband, is a frequent visitor to their house. He hopes to seduce Hedda

Mrs Tanqueray: character in *The Second Mrs Tanqueray* (1893) by Arthur Wing Pinero (1855-1934), a successful English dramatist

Saint Teresa (or Theresa) of Avila: a Spanish nun (1515-1582) who founded the reformed order of Carmelites. She was canonised (made a saint in the Roman Catholic Church) in 1622. A famous work by Bernini depicts the ecstasy of Saint Theresa

odalisque: female slave or concubine

cadi: the judge of a Persian, Arab or Turkish town or village

***The Arabian Nights*:** the celebrated medieval Arabic collection of stories (also called *The Thousand and One Nights*) in which Scheherazade avoids death by telling one tale after another to the Sultan

The Old Maids of England: a song

The Arabian storyteller: a reference to the anonymous author of *The Arabian Nights*

the ... gospels:	the four books of the New Testament supposed to have been written by the Saints Matthew, Mark, Luke and John
Martin Luther:	a German monk (1483–1546) who preached in the Catholic Church, came into conflict with it and broke away to become one of the most influential early Protestants
H. G. Wells's *War of the Worlds*:	H. G. Wells (1866–1946) was a Fabian, like Shaw, and was a well-known novelist. His *The War of the Worlds* was published in 1898
Bostonian Utopia:	an utopia (derived from Greek: no place, hence not a real but an ideal society so named because Sir Thomas More's *Utopia* (1516) described such a society) set in Boston, a city in the Eastern United States
Fourier:	Charles Fourier (1772–1837), a French utopian socialist
Owen:	Robert Owen (1771–1858) an English industrialist and reformer, started an utopian community called New Harmony in 1825 in Indiana, USA
millennial colonies:	ideal communities or utopias
Paolo and Francesca:	lovers whose tragic story is recalled by Dante (1265–1321), the great Italian poet, in *The Divine Comedy* (1321)
Punch:	a puppet with a huge nose and chin famous in the Punch and Judy shows for children. The character developed from the Italian Pulcinella
Lamarckian adaptation:	the idea of the French evolutionist, Jean Baptiste Lamarck (1744–1829), that animals change their organs and thus adapt themselves over the years as their needs change. Evolution is seen as a series of responses to changing conditions
Beatrices:	Beatrice was the lady whom Dante saw once and thereafter loved. He celebrated her in his *Divine Comedy*
Kaisers:	the Kaiser (the Roman Caesar) was the title used by kings in the Holy Roman Empire, Austria and Germany
playing to the gallery:	acting which aims to please by crude effects. The gallery contains the cheapest seats in the theatre, near the roof and far away from the stage
led by the nose:	an idiom meaning to be led astray or deceived
Milton, John:	English poet and puritan (1608–1674), author of *Paradise Lost*, a great Christian epic poem

Cromwell, Oliver: (1599–1658) the military and political leader who won the English Civil War for the puritan side, deposing King Charles I and becoming Lord Protector of the Commonwealth (1653–58)

Bunyan, John: English preacher and author (1628–88) of *Pilgrim's Progress*, a Christian allegory

realists: here the term means those who do not deceive themselves by illusions or false ideals

Philistine: having no interest in art and no cultivated taste

Bismarckian: following the attitudes or ideas of Otto von Bismarck (1815–98), the first Chancellor of the German Empire, who was known as 'the Iron Chancellor'

diabolonian ethics: the name Shaw gives to his ideas of conduct which are contrary to many of the conventional ideas of behaviour in English society at the beginning of this century. He links his ethics to the diabolonian or devilish in order to show that he is opposed to conventional and often hypocritical ethics

Cervantes, Miguel de: Spanish author (1547–1616) of *Don Quixote*, a celebrated comic and satirical book

Royal Academy: English society of artists for supporting art. The Royal Academy holds a yearly exhibition of paintings by its members

H. R. H.: abbreviation for His (or Her) Royal Highness

***Quintessence of Ibsenism*:** a book (1891) by Shaw giving his view of the plays and ideas of Henrik Ibsen

Schopenhauer, Arthur: a German philosopher (1788–1860) who emphasised the importance of the human will

So-and-So: colloquial phrase used when the speaker has forgotten a person's name, or as in this case wishes the reader to think of any appropriate person to fit the context. Compare such phrases as 'what's-his-name' or 'such and such'

a motley: a fool, clown or jester, so-called because the traditional jester's multi-coloured costume was known as 'motley'

Dryden, John: English satirical poet and dramatist (1631–1700). He was also a major critic and prose writer

Wagner, Richard: German composer and writer (1813–83), celebrated for his music-drama, especially his *Ring* cycle based on Nordic myth

The cart and trumpet: self-advertisement and loud explanations in the manner of a tradesman or hawker selling his goods

Summaries · 21

The Devil's Disciple: this play (1877) by Shaw was a success in America, making Shaw rich enough to live entirely by his writing
Adelphi: a London theatre
Mansfield, Richard: successful American actor (1854–1907) who ran his own company after 1886 and produced many plays, including Shaw's *The Devil's Disciple* and *Caesar and Cleopatra*
Robert Buchanan: a dramatist (1841–1901)
Cool as a Cucumber: a farce (1851) by W. B. Jerrold (1826–84)
Byron-Robertson school: the writers and plays using the manner and techniques of these nineteenth century playwrights
Arms and the Man: Shaw's play (1894) was produced at the Avenue Theatre
G.B.S.: Shaw, after he became famous, was often referred to simply by his initials
Flying Dutchman: a legendary sailor supposed to sail the seas in a ghostly ship until the end of time
claptraps: tricks by which a playwright wins easy applause
Buckstone's *Wreck Ashore*: *The Wreck Ashore* (1856) was by one of the most prolific writers of farce in London, J. B. Buckstone (1802–79)
A. B. Walkley: English dramatic critic (1855–1926) who wrote for *The Times* (1900–26). He published *Frames of Mind* in 1899
Dick Dudgeon: the hero of Shaw's *The Devil's Disciple*
Dickens, Charles: world famous English novelist (1812–70). He published *Little Dorrit* in 1855–7
Mrs Dudgeon: Dick Dudgeon's mother in Shaw's play
Mrs Gargery: a character in Charles Dickens's novel, *Great Expectations* (1860–1)
Prometheus: in Greek myth a cunning brother of the giant Atlas. Prometheus made a man and woman of clay and brought them to life with fire stolen from the gods. He was punished by Zeus who chained him to a rock where an eagle ate his liver each day. Each night his liver grew again
Wagnerian Siegfried: Siegfried or Sigurd was a Nordic hero whose Legend forms part of Wagner's opera cycle, *The Ring of the Nibelung*
the Superman: the idea of a bold, new heroic man who goes beyond conventional morality in Nietzsche's philosophical work *Thus Spake Zarathustra*
Blake, William: English poet, engraver and visionary (1757–1827)

Marriage of Heaven and Hell: a work by Blake which reverses orthodox values

Nietzsche, Friedrich: German philosopher (1844–1900) and friend at one time of Wagner

Good and Evil: a reference to Nietzsche's new interpretation of these terms in his work, *Beyond Good and Evil* (trans. 1891)

Murray Carson: an actor, dramatist and producer (1865–1917)

Forbes Robertson: Sir Johnston Forbes-Robertson (1853–1937) was an actor-manager remembered also for his playing of Hamlet, Shakespeare's famous tragic Prince. He produced *Caesar and Cleopatra* at the Savoy Theatre in 1907, nine years after it was written

Lady Cicely Waynflete: a character in Shaw's play, *Captain Brassbound's Conversion*

Circe: an enchantress in Homer's *Odyssey* who changes some of Odysseus's men into pigs

Vanity of vanities: a reference to Ecclesiastes 1:2 in the Bible

Thackeray: William Makepeace Thackeray (1811–63) a satirical English novelist, author of *Vanity Fair* (1847–8)

baying the moon: idiom based on the howls of dogs or wolves; it suggests that those who preach the futility of human actions and desires do so in vain, because people always ignore them

Out, out, brief candle!: words spoken by Macbeth when he muses on his wife's death (Shakespeare: *Macbeth*, Act V Scene 3)

Trumpery moral kitchen scales: Shaw compares cheap kitchen scales, inadequate for a really big scientific task, to a set of moral conventions inadequate for dealing with life

Hogarth: William Hogarth (1697–1764), painter and engraver, satirised aspects of eighteenth century English life through sets of pictures. His most well-known are *The Rake's Progress* and *The Harlot's Progress*, which depict the evils of debauchery

Swift: Jonathan Swift (1667–1745), Dean of St Patrick's, Dublin, and one of the great Anglo-Irish writers. In his satire, *Gulliver's Travels* (1726), Lemuel Gulliver visits Brobdingnag, a land of giants. The King, after listening to Gulliver's account of English and European society, concludes that 'the bulk of your natives are the most pernicious race of little odious vermin that Nature ever suffered to crawl upon the surface of the earth.' In the fourth book, Gulliver reaches a land of filthy brutish men called Yahoos

	governed by horse-creatures called Houynhnyms who govern with superior rationality, though without sentiment. This idea may have been suggested to Swift by the legend that the Roman Emperor, Caligula, once made a horse a member of the Senate
Strindberg:	August Strindberg (1849–1912) was a Swedish dramatist of genius; Shaw used his Nobel prize money in 1925 to support English translations of Swedish literature, starting with Strindberg's plays
The flight of angels sing thee to thy rest:	Shaw misquotes Horatio's lines over the corpse of Hamlet, his friend and Prince: 'Good-night sweet prince, and flights of angels sing thee to thy rest! . .' (*Hamlet*, Act V Scene 2)
Adsum:	(*Latin*) I am present
maudlin:	grossly or excessively sentimental
Tea-drunkards:	Shaw disliked tea. The phrase jokingly contradicts the famous description of tea as 'the cup/That cheer but not inebriate' by the English poet William Cowper (1731–1800)
Mrs Quickly:	Mistress Quickly was hostess of the Boar's Head Tavern, Eastcheap, London. She appears in Shakespeare's *Henry IV*, *Henry V* and *The Merry Wives of Windsor*
Actium:	a place in Greece where Octavian defeated Antony and Cleopatra's forces in 31BC
bawdry:	bawdy or indecent jokes and actions
drabbing:	seeking the company of drabs or whores
Lear:	the aged king in Shakespeare's great tragedy *King Lear* (1605–6)
Brutus:	a character in Shakespeare's *Julius Caesar* (1599–1600)
Girondin:	taking their name from the Gironde region of France, the Girondins were moderates in the French Revolution and many were guillotined by extremists. Shakespeare's Brutus is a moderate. Little is known of the historical Brutus, but he killed himself after his defeat by Antony and Octavian
Dr Johnson:	Dr Samuel Johnson (1709–1784) compiled a celebrated dictionary and wrote poetry, plays and some of the best criticism of the eighteenth century
utterances of Napoleon:	the French soldier and Emperor, Napoleon I, during his Egyptian campaign made a speech to his army before the pyramids

Ben Jonson: English playwright and poet (1572–1637) who was a friend of Shakespeare

Frank Harris: British author and editor (1856–1931) who wrote *The Man Shakespeare* (1909)

Elizabeth's time: refers to Queen Elizabeth I (1533–1603) of England

Garrick, David: English actor-manager and dramatist (1717–79) famed for his acting of Shakespeare's tragic and comic roles

Cibber, Colley: English dramatist, theatre manager and actor (1671–1757). He led the fashion for sentimental comedy which replaced the bawdier restoration drama

Coliseum: a London theatre named after the Roman Colosseum or amphitheatre of Vespasian used for spectacular entertainments

Augustin Daly: American theatre-manager (1831–99) who, like some English managers, produced mangled versions of Shakespeare's plays

Gloster: character in Shakespeare's *King Lear* who is blinded. His story forms a sub-plot which ironically reflects the main plot of Lear's sufferings

Fortinbras: a minor character in Shakespeare's *Hamlet* whose extreme honour ironically reflects on Hamlet's situation and reluctance to shed blood

Benson: Sir Frank Robert Benson (1858–1939), English actor-manager, famed for his Shakespeare touring company and productions at Stratford-upon-Avon. He was knighted by King George V in the Theatre Royal, Drury Lane

Polonius: in *Hamlet*, the King's adviser and father of Ophelia; Polonius is killed in error by Hamlet

Bardolatry: worship of the Bard as an idol—hence excessive and uncritical praise of Shakespeare

***Peer Gynt*:** a poetic drama (1867) by Henrik Ibsen in which the hero travels on a voyage of self-discovery

***Don Giovanni*:** the opera (1787) by W. A. Mozart (1756–91) in which the Don is punished for his lechery by being dragged into hell by the stone statue of a man he has killed

The Niblung's Ring: Shaw's eccentric spelling of *The Niebelung's Ring*, a group or cycle of four music-dramas by the German composer, Richard Wagner (1813–83)

Stuart-Glennie: John Stuart Stuart-Glennie wrote *Pilgrim Memories* (1875)

Goethe:	Johann Wolfgang von Goethe (1749–1832), a great German writer most famous for his long two-part work in dramatic form, *Faust* (Part I, 1808; Part II, 1832)
frescoes:	watercolour paintings done on walls before the plaster or mortar has dried
Michael Angelo:	full name Michelangelo Buonarroti (1475–1564); Italian sculptor, painter, architect and poet of the High Renaissance, who painted the Sistine Chapel ceiling in Rome
Raphael:	another Italian Renaissance painter (1483–1520) and architect of genius
Townley mysteries:	plays preserved in a manuscript once possessed by the Towneley family. These thirty-two anonymous plays make up a cycle depicting episodes from the Bible
Giotto:	full name Giotto di Bondone (1276?–1337?); a Florentine painter, architect and sculptor
Byron, George Gordon:	Lord Byron, sixth Baron of Rochdale (1788–1824); English poet with satirical wit, an influential figure in the development of European romanticism
William Morris:	English poet, designer and socialist (1834–96)
Beethoven, Ludwig van:	German composer (1770–1827) of much sublime music including the Ninth (or 'Choral') symphony and the opera, *Fidelio*
Swinburne, Algernon Charles:	English poet (1837–1909) who wrote a tragedy in the classical manner, *Atalanta in Calydon* (1865) as well as much poetry and criticism
Stevenson, Robert Louis:	Scottish novelist and poet (1850–1894), famous for his adventure stories, *Treasure Island* and *Kidnapped*
Scott, Sir Walter:	Scottish novelist and poet (1771–1832) celebrated for his historical novels
Mendelssohn, Felix:	German composer, conductor and pianist (1809–1847)
Maclise, Daniel:	Maclise (1806–1870) published the Maclise portrait gallery of illustrious literary characters. This was reissued in 1898
Madox Brown:	a British painter (1821–93) whose style anticipated and inspired D. G. Rossetti and other Pre-Raphaelite painters
Rienzi, Coladi:	Italian patriot (1313?–1354) who was assassinated. Wagner's opera *Rienzi* (1842) was an early work

Zastrozzi: a romance by Shelley, published when he was an Oxford student
Rossini, Gioacchino Antonio: Italian composer (1792–1868) of opera and sacred music
Spontini, Gasparo Luigi Pacifico: Italian composer (1774–1851)
Meyerbeer, Giacomo: German composer (1791–1864) of opera
Moore, Thomas: Irish poet and satirist (1779–1852)
Homer: The name by which we know an ancient Greek epic poet, or group of poets, living in the eighth century BC who wrote the *Iliad* and *Odyssey*, epic poems about the Trojan War and the wanderings of Odysseus
Achilles: bravest of the Greeks in the Trojan War, he was almost proof against all injury because his mother, Thetis, plunged him into the magical river Styx when he was an infant. His heel by which she held him was not touched by the waters. He was wounded in the heel and died
Ajax: next to Achilles, the bravest of the warriors in the Trojan War. After the death of Achilles, Ajax and Ulysses quarrelled over who should have the dead hero's weapons
Troilus and Cressida: play by Shakespeare concerning the Trojan War, written in 1601–2
Henry V: Henry V (1387–1422) reigned as King of England from 1413, defeating the French in 1415 at the battle of Agincourt. He married Catherine de Valois
Mommsen: Theodor Mommsen (1817–1903) wrote a history of ancient Rome. His account of Julius Caesar influenced Shaw's conception of him
Vercingetorix: a chief of the Gauls in the time of Julius Caesar
Carlyle, Thomas: Scottish historian and writer (1795–1881)
preux chevalier: *(French)* brave knight
Cervantes, Miguel de: Spanish writer (1547–1616) famous for his *Don Quixote* (1605–15)
Plutarchian: in the manner of Plutarch (AD45-*c*.125), the Greek writer whose *Parallel Lives of Greeks and Romans*, translated by Sir Thomas North in 1579, was used by Shakespeare as a source for his Roman plays
Marlowe's Tamerlane: Christopher Marlowe (1564–93), Shakespeare's contemporary and rival as a playwright, was stabbed to death in a tavern. *Tamburlaine* (Parts I and II) traced the rise and fall of this great and ruthless warrior

Harlequin, columbine, clown and pantaloon: Harlequin (Arlecchino, one of the most celebrated of the characters in Italian comedy), Columbine (Columbina, the heroine's maid), the clown (Zanni, usually a valet and trickster), and pantaloon (Pantalone, or comic old man, usually a parent or guardian) are figures from the Commedia dell'Arte, a type of partly improvised comedy which flourished in Italy from the sixteenth century onwards

Cyrano's nose: Cyrano de Bergerac (1619–55), French swordsman and writer; his enormous nose and hopeless love for his beautiful cousin were the subject of Edmond Rostand's extravagantly theatrical play, *Cyrano de Bergerac* (1898)

Marx, (Heinrich) Karl: German political and economic philosopher (1818–83) who, from 1849 until his death, lived and wrote in London. His *Communist Manifesto* (1848) and *Capital* (3 Vols: 1869, 1885 and 1895) written with Friedrich Engels (1820–95) have had a profound influence on socialists ever since

Mill, John Stuart: English economist and political theorist (1806–73) famous for his essay *On Liberty* and his *Autobiography*

Plato: Greek philosopher (*c.*428–347BC), pupil of Socrates (469–399BC) and author of many philosophical books in dialogue form, such as *The Phaedo*, *The Symposium* and *The Republic*

Prologue

The Temple of Ra in Memphis, capital of ancient Egypt. Out of the gloom, the mysteriously shining figure of the god Ra speaks directly to the audience. His speech mocks the audience and criticises the London theatre of Shaw's youth and middle-age. He tells the audience that modern man is as foolish as ancient man, and that the British Empire is not as solid or enduring as the Egyptian one, whose pyramids still stand.

The prologue explains that ancient history is very like our own age. England changed from an old to a new society, much as Rome changed from a small but aggressive capitalist state into an imperial power, exploiting its colonies by means of capitalism.

Ra recalls the historical events which are the background to the play, such as Caesar's pursuit of Pompey to Egypt, and the killing of Pompey by 'his old comrade' Lucius Septimus. We are told that the play is for our education. It is not the story of Cleopatra's sexual life. Ra's final satirical remark is that we are too dull to learn from his teaching, but he asks us to settle down and watch the play.

NOTES AND GLOSSARY:

Ra: hawk-headed Egyptian sun-god, much represented in ancient sculpture and wall-painting

Memphis: in ancient times the capital of Egypt, it is south of modern Cairo

Be silent and hearken unto me: the archaic language is used as a convention to show that it is a god who speaks. The human characters all speak modern English. This makes them seem very much like us, which is precisely what Shaw wants us to think. Shaw is also making fun here of the restlessness of audiences at the beginning of a performance

ye quaint little islanders: those who live in the British Isles. The phrase reminds us of Swift's famous satire of the English in *Gulliver's Travels*, where human beings are seen as essentially small and petty

Give ear: Listen

ye men with white paper on your breasts: a reference to the starched dress shirts worn with evening dress by gentlemen sitting in the dress circle seats of the theatre

packed in rows ... obstructing one another's vision: a joke about the many uncomfortable seats in theatres where the floor of the auditorium is not raked (sloped) steeply enough to prevent the nuisance of others' heads blocking one's view

Let not your men speak nor your women cough: a joke at the expense of noisy and restless audiences slow to settle down

ye compulsorily educated ones: a reference to the Education Act of 1870 which made education compulsory for all up to fourteen years of age. The age limit has since been raised to sixteen

old Rome and a new: Ancient Rome was first a small republic, but then became a vast Empire ruled by Emperors. Similarly, puritan England was briefly a Republic under Cromwell, and began to accumulate a vast empire after the restoration of the monarchy

Caesar: Gaius Julius Caesar (100–44 BC) a Roman soldier and statesman, who defeated Pompey in civil war to become ruler of Rome. He was assassinated by Brutus, Cassius and others on 15 March

that cad among gods, Mammon: a god of money in the ancient world, Mammon is here called a cad for satirical effect. 'Cad' was a popular term for an unprincipled and selfish person with a veneer of gentlemanly habits. Jesus warned 'Ye cannot serve both God and Mammon.' (Matthew 6:24)

your fleet that covers thirty miles of the sea: the British navy which in 1912 was the largest in the world

the field of Pharsalia: the battlefield where Julius Caesar defeated Pompey in Thessaly, Greece in 48 BC

blood and iron: a reference to Bismarck's famous speech to the Prussian House of Deputies (28 January 1886) in which he called for massive armaments and a policy of war succeeding through 'Blut und Eisen' (blood and iron)

imperial Spain crumbled: the small English fleet fighting against great odds defeated the powerful Spanish Armada in the English Channel in 1588

there was but now a British one: refers to the British occupation of Egypt

distraint: an order to pay tax or tribute, usually of goods or money

Lucius Septimius: little is known about him. Plutarch merely tells us he was once an Officer of Pompey, but Shaw makes him figure significantly in the play

story of an unchaste woman: Shaw uses the popular notion that Cleopatra was beautiful and promiscuous in order to satirise audiences who like plays dealing only with illicit sexual love

An alternative to the Prologue

It is dawn on an October night in 48BC on the border of Egypt with Syria. The soldiers in the palace are either listening to dirty jokes or gambling with their captain, Belzanor, and a sly young recruit, a Persian. The moment after the Persian wins, the gaming is interrupted by the arrival of Bel Affris, a guard from the temple of Ra, loyal neither to Cleopatra nor Ptolemy. Coming wounded from battle, he tells how his company encountered fleeing Egyptians defeated by Caesar's Legions. He describes Roman tactics in the battle so vividly that the Egyptians' contempt for the Romans is quickly replaced by respect and even fear, in the case of one of the sentinals. He flings down his javelin and escapes into the palace to spread the news that the victorious Romans are only one hour away. The others discuss what is to be done with Cleopatra and her retinue of women. The cunning Persian advises that Cleopatra be sold to her brother Ptolemy as a prisoner, that Caesar be told of her beauty and then urged to lead Egyptians and Romans together to rescue her. Belzanor and his men would thus become the Queen's guard. She would reign with Caesar over Egypt after Ptolemy's defeat.

The guards surround the doors of the palace to prevent the escape of the servants, and Belzanor demands to see the Queen's nurse, Ftatateeta. Her entry is impressive because of her appearance. Enormous, grim and incredibly strong, she is insolent, arrogant and contemptuous of others because she rules the Queen. She is unimpressed by news of the Romans and reveals that Cleopatra has been missing since the previous evening. Belzanor, refusing to believe her, tells the Persian to kill Ftatateeta. He orders a search for the Queen. Ftatateeta is unafraid to die and still contemptuous. She reveals that Cleopatra feels the only power greater than Caesar's or Ftatateeta's is that of the Sphinx, and that they should seek the Queen there. The Persian sees this advice as a plot to send the Egyptians to clash with the Roman soldiers. But as he decides to kill the old nurse, she trips him and escapes. There is general confusion as fugitives and guardsmen rush in a panic from the palace, revealing that Cleopatra and her sacred white cat have gone.

NOTES AND GLOSSARY:

The XXXIII Dynasty: Ancient Egypt was governed by dynasties or lines of hereditary rulers. Ptolemy I, a general of Alexander the Great, established the Ptolemaic or XXXIII Dynasty in 323BC. This was the year of 706 in the Roman calendar.

Buckingham Palace: since 1837 when Victoria became Queen of England, this palace has been the London residence of the British monarch. Shaw disliked its architecture, and as a socialist and Irishman disapproved of it as a symbol of British Imperialism

the Mahdi: Mohammed Ahmed (1843–85), assumed this title, meaning guide appointed by God, to lead the forces of Islam. In 1881 he rebelled against the government in the Sudan. He besieged and captured Khartoum, killing the British commander, General Gordon, in 1885

subalterns: in using this rank from the modern British army, Shaw is deliberately anachronistic, in accord with his theory that human affairs are essentially the same in every period

Nubian: a black native of Nubia, enslaved by the Egyptians at one time

Summaries · 31

Apis:	Egyptian god in the form of a sacred bull
Double or quits:	phrase used when gambling by tossing a coin to see which side falls face upwards. If a player calls correctly he need not pay what he owes, being therefore 'quit' of his debt; but a wrong call means that he must pay double what he originally owed to his opponent
descended from the gods:	alludes to the custom in ancient times among some people of rank to derive their ancestry from gods
Ptolemy:	the name of the dynasty of Egyptian rulers from 323–30BC. The boy king takes his name from this dynasty
papyrus:	a kind of paper made in ancient times from the stem of the papyrus plant
The battle was not to the strong; but the race was to the swift:	here Shaw wittily adapts the proverbial phrase from the Bible, Ecclesiastes 9:11, 'the race is not to the swift, nor the battle to the strong.' This and a few other archaisms in the dialogue give the impression of speakers from the ancient world
crupper:	a strap which loops around a horse's tail and which stops the saddle from slipping forward; also the croup or hindquarters of a horse
Cleopatra is descended from the river Nile:	life in Egypt largely depended on the irrigation of the land by the River Nile, which thus seemed to be a divine source of life and was worshipped as a god
Osiris:	an ancient Egyptian god whose yearly death and resurrection acted out the fertility of nature, bursting into life again each spring after the winter
Sphinx:	a figure with a human head and lion's body. The most famous one is the Great Sphinx at Giza which guards the Nile Valley

Act I

A magical harp plays as the moon rises over the desert to reveal the Sphinx. Cleopatra is asleep, hiding behind its paws. Enter Caesar. He addresses the Sphinx as if it were an equal. Caesar's monologue (a long speech uninterrupted by other speakers) begins with his ideas that he is greater than all other men and equal to the Sphinx in importance. Yet he is its opposite in many respects.

At just this moment Cleopatra, who has awakened and listened to

Caesar for a while, suddenly calls out to him 'Old gentleman'. The effect is comic; Caesar at first thinks that the Sphinx is talking to him. He soon learns that it is Cleopatra, though she does not learn his identity. She invites him to climb up and hide from the Romans with her, for she is lonely. She reveals that her sacred white cat has run away with a black cat, possibly her great-great-great grandmother. Her superstitions and the legendary account of her ancestry from the union of the black cat and the River Nile add to Caesar's feeling that he is living a remarkable dream.

Cleopatra tells Caesar that she plans to kill her brother, move into the palace at Alexandria and do whatever pleases her. Caesar treats her as a child and wonders why she is not at home in bed. She is afraid of the Romans, believing they are barbarians who eat their captives, and that Caesar's 'father was a tiger and his mother a burning mountain, and his nose is like an elephant's trunk'. She believes all Romans to be monstrous.

Caesar seems even more certain this can only be a dream, so Cleopatra jabs his arm with a hair pin. Angered by this, Caesar decides to go back to his camp. But he first draws her attention to his Roman features, and she prays that the Sphinx 'bite him in two.' He now teases her again by warning her that Caesar might eat her. He also begins to teach her how to be a monarch. His first lesson is that she must hide her fear of Caesar.

They hear another blast of the bucina. As the Romans approach, Caesar and Cleopatra steal back into the palace to the throne room. Now Caesar builds up her confidence to give orders to servants, even the formidable Ftatateeta. Caesar shows that he can control the aggressive old nurse by the power of his commanding personality, and his willingness to use the slave as an executioner if necessary. These first lessons in becoming a ruler excite Cleopatra to a childish display of power when she beats her slave. She jumps to the throne, shouting that she is at last a real queen. Caesar is worried about Egypt's future under the rule of such a queen. Cleopatra hugs him, planning to make her lovers kings, and, when she tires of them, to whip them to death. He predicts that she 'will be the most dangerous of all Caesar's conquests.'

The mention of Caesar brings back her fear: she wants to run and hide. Caesar now gives her the next lesson in royal behaviour. He convinces her that she must put on her queenly garb, compose herself and act with courage fitting for a queen, for Caesar 'will know Cleopatra by her pride, her courage, her majesty and her beauty.' Cleopatra denies she is trembling with fear. Her women dress her in royal robes and Caesar puts the crown upon her head, asking whether it is 'sweet or bitter to be a queen.' She replies honestly with one word, 'Bitter!' Caesar urges her to cast out fear. We learn that the guards have fled; another

Nubian dashes in with news that the Romans are in the courtyard. The women flee, save for Ftatateeta and Cleopatra, who, held by Caesar, suppresses her fear. She resolves to face Caesar. Ftatateeta encourages her to be brave and keep her word, even if it means death. Caesar leads her back towards the throne, and sits on it himself as the Romans march in, get into line and salute him. Cleopatra suddenly realises who her 'old king' is, and ends the act by sobbing with relief as she 'falls into his arms.'

NOTES AND GLOSSARY:

Memnon: the legendary statue of King Amenhotep or Amenophis III at Thebes which gave out music when the sun's rays passed over it. Shaw alters the legend by stressing the moon in place of the sun, and replacing the statue with 'the windswept harp'. This recalls the aeolian harp of Greek mythology, which played by itself when the wind blew over it

bellow of a Minotaur: the mythical beast of King Minos of Crete. The Minotaur, a bull-like monster connected with the bull cult of the Minoans, lived in a labyrinth where he killed young men and women from Greece who were sacrificed to him each year. The bellow in Shaw's stage directions refers to the sound of the Roman Bucina or war trumpet, which he is really comparing to the fearful sound of the Minotaur

Gaul, Britain, Spain, Thessaly: all were provinces of the Roman Empire. Gaul signified the country known now as France. Thessaly was part of Greece

Queen of the Gypsies: Caesar calls her this because gypsies or Romanies were (wrongly) supposed to have originally come from Egypt. Ironically, Cleopatra could just as wrongly call Caesar King of the Romanies, linking them with Rome! Actually, these wanderers who live as tinkers, have a 'king' and a language known as Romany, are said to originate in Roumania

ensign with his eagle: the soldier carrying a carved Roman eagle as the sign or standard of the legion

transept: a passage or aisle, usually running at a right angle from the nave in a Christian church, but here used to mean just a spacious walk-way or corridor in the palace

dress into ordered rank: the movement in army drill by which soldiers form straight lines by raising an arm to touch the shoulder of the next man in the line, until all are one arm's length away from each other

Act II

The setting is a hall on the first floor of the royal palace in Alexandria. It is a sunny morning. At the top of the loggia steps is a ten-year-old boy, King Ptolemy Dionysus, with his guardian, the eunuch Pothinus, who leads him by the hand before the assembly of courtiers. In a group of Ptolemy's right is Theodotus, his tutor, while in a group on his left is his general, Achillas.

When Ptolemy reaches the chair of state, he addresses the court. Prompted by Pothinus, the boy-king in a toneless voice falters his way through a badly memorised speech, claiming that the gods will punish Cleopatra by causing her to be executed, because she plans to take the throne. He adds that she has bewitched Caesar with the help of Ftatateeta. He forgets to add that no foreigner will be allowed to control the throne of Egypt. Achillas's news that Caesar has only 3000 soldiers and about 1000 horsemen makes the court laugh with scorn at Roman power.

Announced by Rufio, Caesar enters with his secretary, Britannus. After brief joking words with Ptolemy, Achillas and Theodotus, Caesar asks for money. Rufio shocks and scares the Egyptians by making the tripod sacred to Ra serve as a seat for Caesar. There is '*a hissing whisper of sacrilege!*' After introducing his companions, Caesar coolly asks for 1600 talents. The courtiers are appalled, and Pothinus protests that the treasury has no such sum in it, that there is the dispute over the throne to be settled between Ptolemy and Cleopatra, that the taxes have not been collected for a year, and that the melting down of gold ornaments and goblets from the court to mint money would make the people angry. Caesar cuts through these arguments by revealing that his officers are already collecting taxes, this being the main business of a conqueror of the world. In return for all the money, Caesar offers to settle the year-old dispute, whether or not Pothinus wishes it. Caesar jokingly calls for 'Totateeta' who enters with Cleopatra. Encouraged to behave as a queen, Cleopatra then drags Ptolemy from the throne and sits there herself. Caesar comforts Ptolemy, who is crying. Cleopatra, suddenly jealous, contemptuously sends Ptolemy back to his throne, declaring she is not afraid of Caesar.

Caesar, Rufio and Britannus are amazed at the custom of the Pharoahs that children of the royal household had to marry each other. Britannus protests it is improper. Caesar asks Theodotus to pardon the Briton who 'thinks that the customs of his tribal island are the laws of nature.' He then suggests a plan for peace. Cleopatra and Ptolemy may rule jointly in Egypt, and their youngest brother and sister must marry, and be given Cyprus to rule over. The plan Britannus labels 'peace with honor' while the courtiers, wishing to settle their disputes themselves, shout 'Egypt for the Egyptians!' Rufio reminds them contemptuously that Romans occupy Egypt. Achillas tries to save his dignity by claiming that he is the general of the Romans in Egypt, much to Caesar's amusement, who jokes that since Achillas is general of both sides, Roman and Egyptian, it would be useful to know which side he is on at present. Achillas replies 'on the side of right and of the gods.'

Now the talk becomes serious: the Egyptians regain their confidence because their army outnumbers the Romans. They decide to arrest Cleopatra and Caesar. Rufio calls in the Roman guards thus making the courtiers Caesar's prisoners. Caesar prefers to call them his 'guests' and then tells them they are free to go. But Pothinus realises Caesar is really turning Ptolemy's courtiers out of their palace, and insists on his right as the King's guardian to stay. Caesar causes a sensation when he says his own right is in Rufio's sword. Pothinus bitterly questions Roman 'justice' and Theodotus reminds Caesar that he should be grateful because the Egyptians refused to harbour Pompey, Caesar's enemy. Pothinus calls in Lucius Septimius, the military tribune, to tell how he beheaded Pompey. Caesar is overcome with emotion, and is horrified at the suggestion that he wished for revenge. But Caesar hates this murder, making a powerful speech against vengeance and his own earlier punishment of Vercingetorix and the Gauls. This prompts him to offer Lucius Septimius freedom or a place in his service. But Lucius, thinking Caesar will be defeated, goes out, followed by Achillas and the other Egyptians except for Ptolemy.

Rufio and Britannus are annoyed that Caesar has not killed his enemies in the interests of his own and Rome's security. Caesar is more concerned to send Ptolemy off to join Pothinus. Cleopatra is hurt to think she might also be sent away, but Caesar, deciding that she should live in state in the palace, orders Ftatateeta to arrange this. Ftatateeta boldly asks to be mistress of the Queen's household. Cleopatra threatens to have her thrown to the crocodiles. When Caesar is shocked, Cleopatra tells him he is sentimental. Amazed by her cheekiness, Caesar rebukes her for thinking she already knows more than he does. He has work to do and she should leave, but she tells him kings do not work. She recalls that her father did not work, but that it was Antony who restored him to the throne. She would like to marry Antony. Caesar tells her he might be able to arrange it. She assumes Antony is many years younger than Caesar. Caesar ruefully answers her excited questions about Antony, including the fact that many women love him. Caesar also tells her that he sent Antony to restore her father to his throne for a fee of 16,000 talents. The debt was never fully paid off.

Caesar again tries to start on his work in order to prevent the Egyptian forces from cutting the Romans off from the harbour. Cleopatra sees the wisdom of this, for she wants to 'keep the way over the seas open for . . .

Mark Antony'. She runs out 'kissing her hand to Mark Antony across the sea'.

Caesar calls for Britannus, but a wounded soldier enters to say that an army commanded by Achillas has arrived, and the citizens are rioting. When Rufio enters, Caesar explains they are beseiged. Caesar orders his men to make for the beach and stand by the boats. He astonishes Rufio by ordering the ships in the west harbour to be burned. Rufio is to take every boat from the east harbour to sieze the Pharos, leaving half the men to hold the beach and the palace quay.

Pothinus is then admitted, for he has been demanding to speak with Caesar, to deliver an ultimatum; Caesar, though, takes him prisoner, and continues to direct the military operations. Theodotus rushes in calling for help to save the library from fire. Caesar is unconcerned. Speaking as an author, he says it is better to live than dream life away with books, that books (even great ones) which do not flatter mankind are destroyed anyway, that history cannot prevent death from sending us all (even great men) to the common grave, that the memory of mankind is shameful and should burn, and that the destruction of the past allows us to 'build the future with its ruins.' Caesar tells Theodotus that since he valued Pompey's head so little, but now pleads 'for a few sheepskins scrawled with errors,' he should go to Achillas's legions to fight the fire. He also sends Pothinus to urge that the Egyptians kill no more Roman soldiers, otherwise Pothinus will be killed. Rufio notices the prisoners have gone, but Caesar explains that each prisoner needs two soldiers as guards.

When Caesar calls again for Britannus to bring his armour, Cleopatra also appears carrying the helmet and sword. When she takes Caesar's laurel wreath to put on his helmet, she laughs to see just how bald he is. As Caesar had mocked books, so Cleopatra now mocks the conqueror's bay leaves as merely a device to hide a bald patch. She tells Caesar a cure for baldness. He is annoyed by her stressing his age, but when Britannus rebukes her, she mocks him for having been dyed blue in accord with the ancient British custom, and buckles on Caesar's sword for him.

Rufio is impatient to get to the ships, but Cleopatra is now worried that Caesar might be killed in battle. Caesar tells her she must learn to watch battles. Cleopatra sees the Egyptian troops, as she thinks, emptying the harbour of water with buckets, but Caesar explains that they are saving the library from fire, and this will occupy them while Caesar captures the lighthouse. Cleopatra waves Caesar an affectionate goodbye.

NOTES AND GLOSSARY:

loggia: a gallery open to one side, and overlooking the land outside, or in this case, the sea

Summaries · 37

theocracy: a state where government is by gods or their priests

in profile as flat ornament: a description of the characteristic art of ancient Egypt as it is found in wall-paintings

Tottenham Court Road: a busy London street (at the end of Oxford Street). Its shops are not as fashionable as some stores in other parts of the West End of London

magpie keenness: magpies, black and white birds about the size of crows, are quick to pick up whatever their sharp eyes take a fancy to; they are fond of glittering objects

leading strings: the halter and short rope sometimes used for walking a horse

Auletes the Flute Blower: Ptolemy XI, an illegitimate son of Ptolemy X

oak wreath: a cluster of oak leaves. Roman headgear of this design was a mark of military honours

talents: coins used in the ancient world

sesterces: a sesterce was a coin used in ancient Rome

sibylline: adjective meaning 'like a Sibyl.' Classical mythology tells of female prophets, called sibyls. The Cumaean Sibyl had the Sibylline Books in which the fate of Rome was written. These were in the Temple of Jupiter, burned down in 83 BC. The stage direction thus suggests that Ftatateeta is an image of mystery and foreboding

Peace with honor: notice Shaw's preference for the older spelling of 'honour' now used in America. The phrase refers to Benjamin Disraeli (1804–81) a famous British Prime Minister and novelist who in July 1878, said in Parliament, 'Lord Salisbury and myself have brought you back peace – but a peace I hope with honour.'

Aulus Gabinius: a Roman military man, Governor of Syria in about 45BC

Cato: Cato the Younger (95–46BC) committed suicide rather than suffer the dishonour of surrender to Caesar

Juba of Numidia: King of Numidia (Northwest Africa) who took his own life for the same reason as Cato

Finnan-haddie: Scottish dialect for Finnan-haddock, a fish smoked over green wood, turf or peat fires, originally in the village of Findhorn. The fish when smoked is a yellowish-brown colour

military tribune: an officer. There were six military tribunes to a Roman legion, each being in command for two months of the year

38 · Summaries

roadstead:	a stretch of water where ships may anchor safely near the shore
Capitol:	the great temple of Jupiter in ancient Rome
porridge:	a breakfast food popular in Britain. It is made from boiled oatmeal
Horus:	Egyptian god of light
the Pharos:	a lighthouse built by Socratus of Cnidus in the third century BC on Pharos, a small island which Alexander the Great joined to the mainland by a road. Fires burned at night on this tower as an aid to shipping. It was destroyed in AD 1375 by an earthquake
the strand:	beach or shore
toga:	the loose outer robe of Roman citizens
The library:	Theodotus is so proud of the great library at Alexandria that he wrongly calls it one of the Seven Wonders of the World
the Seven Wonders of the World:	these were the Pharos, the Colossus of Rhodes (a statue of Apollo), the statue of Zeus by Phidias, the pyramids of Giza, the Temple of Artemis at Ephesus, the tomb of King Mausolus of Caria at Halicarnassus and the Hanging Gardens of Babylon. All have been destroyed, except the pyramids
cuirass and greaves:	the breast and back armour strapped around the body was the cuirass. Greaves were pieces of armour to protect the legs
strong spirits of sugar:	rum. In his notes to the play Shaw has fun with the Queen's cure for baldness
painted all over blue:	ancient Britons used a blue body dye called 'woad'
Britannicus:	this is a joke against his slave, for Britannicus would mean not from Britain, but conqueror of Britain

Act III

A Roman sentry guards the quay in front of the palace. We can see the harbour and the lighthouse in the background. Apollodorus, a Sicilian dandy about twenty-four years old, approaches and stops near him; Ftatateeta and four porters carrying rolls of carpet reach the steps of the palace before stopping to rest.

Apollodorus challenges the guard, making him start with surprise. The sentry challenges Apollodorus, giving him the opportunity to identify himself and reply that his group has already passed by three other sentinels, also too busy to challenge him. Defensively, the guard explains that the orders were to watch the sea. He then notices Ftatateeta, asking insultingly who she is, and also questioning Apollodorus about the carpets. Apollodorus explains that the carpets are for Cleopatra, he being no ordinary merchant, but a patrician and aesthete or one who worships beauty. 'My calling is to choose beautiful things for beautiful queens. My motto is Art for Art's sake.'

The sentinel thinking this is a false password refuses to let him pass, whereupon Ftatateeta, just as the sentry is about to attack, pinions his arms to his sides so that Apollodorus may slit his throat. Apollodorus treats the incident as a joke, and two Roman soldiers who run up with a centurion, free the sentry. The Centurion, to the dismay of Apollodorus, thinks Ftatateeta may be the young man's wife, but he allows the party and their carpets entry to the Queen, as long as only they come out again. Cleopatra is not to leave the palace.

Cleopatra calls to her nurse from the window and comes down to meet her. Ftatateeta disapproves, because it exposes the Queen to the gaze of men. Cleopatra can think only of her need for a boat. She even ignores the Persian carpets. Apollodorus hails a boatman immediately, thus securing Cleopatra's future orders for carpets. The sentinel refuses to allow Cleopatra to embark. Apollodorus challenges the soldier to a duel. The sentry flings his pilum or javelin but Apollodorus nimbly ducks and lunges into a sword fight with the guard, who immediately shouts for help.

The re-entry of the Centurion with several men stops the fight. He, too, refuses to allow Cleopatra to go to Caesar. Apollodorus, declaring that 'who says artist, says duellist', threatens the Centurion with a fight because of the denial of Cleopatra's wishes. Further, he suggests that he should go to Caesar with a present—the richest of the carpets—and return with an order allowing Cleopatra access to Caesar and the Pharos. The Centurion posts two extra men outside the palace, leaving orders that only Apollodorus and his goods may leave. When he has gone, Apollodorus unsuccessfully attempts to bribe the guards. He repeats his offer to get a message to Caesar. Cleopatra then conceives her plan to hide inside a rolled carpet. She does not mention the plan, but gets Apollodorus to promise that a carpet would be handled by the porters very gently indeed. Cleopatra, Ftatateeta and the porters go into the palace to prepare Caesar's present, leaving Apollodorus outside with the sentries.

Apollodorus notices that the Egyptian forces are preparing to attack the Pharos by land and sea. He delights in alerting the slow-witted soldiers to this alarm and calling for the Centurion, who quickly sends the two auxiliaries off to spread the alarm, leaves one man to guard the palace and rushes off with his other guard. The bucina sounds.

The four porters appear carrying a rolled carpet and followed by

Ftatateeta. In a brief comic scene, the carpet is put into the boat and Apollodorus embarks for the lighthouse. It is only when he finds Ftatateeta praying that Cleopatra will be safe, that the guard realises he has been tricked.

At the Pharos, Rufio is enjoying a meal of dates and wine, while Caesar anxiously looks out to sea. Britannus emerges from the lighthouse door, reporting that the tower is about two hundred feet tall, and that one old Tyrian and his fourteen-year-old son operate the crane (for hauling up fuel) by means of counter weights and a steam engine of sorts. He goes off to meet messengers approaching along the mole. Caesar moodily contemplates defeat and Rufio persuades him to take some dates. Britannus rushes in with a bag of captured letters revealing Pompey's allies in the army of occupation. Caesar dumbfounds him by throwing them into the sea, preferring to take no revenge, but win friends by success. British seriousness and moralistic attitudes are satirised by Caesar's flippant behaviour.

Apollodorus arrives with the carpet. Caesar orders him back to Alexandria, but he complains that a fool threw a heavy bag into the boat, damaging it. The crane swings the carpet on to the stage and Caesar discovers Cleopatra inside. Caesar is glad to see her, but warns her that in battle he must value his soldiers who trust him in the face of death more than he can value her. Cleopatra weeps, and Caesar orders Apollodorus to take her back to the palace. But Britannus reports that the Egyptians have landed on the mole between the lighthouse and the Roman barricade, thus cutting Caesar off from the rest of his force.

Apollodorus promises to swim to a galley a quarter of a mile away and send a boat to rescue Caesar's party. He dives into the sea, and Caesar, excited by his boldness, follows him, ordering Cleopatra to be thrown into the sea as well. Britannus, unable to swim, is left behind, but Caesar promises to rescue him. Britannus cheers as the boat reaches the swimmers.

NOTES AND GLOSSARY:
mole: the five-mile-long causeway or Heptastadium which joins the Pharos to the main land
cresset beacon: a metal basket made to contain fiery coals or other burning material. Placed on the top of the tower, the fire could be seen over a great distance
pilum: Roman spear
aestheticism: the cult of beauty in art, where the pursuit of beauty is seen as the only real duty of the artist. This notion was fiercely contested in the 1890s and afterwards
filigree: intricate ornamental work, usually of gold or silver wire

truck:	a wheeled platform or barrow for carrying heavy loads
patrician:	an upper-class Roman, as opposed to a plebeian or commoner
scullions:	servants employed to do simple tasks in a kitchen, such as cleaning and carrying things
squab faced:	fat-faced
faggot:	a bundle
coping:	the top part of a wall, often sloping

Act IV

Six months later, Cleopatra's boudoir in the palace one afternoon in March, 47BC. The Queen sits with her women listening to a slave-girl play the harp. Cleopatra interrupts the music to ask the harpist's master for lessons. The old man assures her that he is superior to all other teachers and that she will take only four years to learn, but must first study Pythagoras. Cleopatra tells him he must teach her as simply as he taught the slave, for she plays better than he does. For every false note Cleopatra plays, he will be flogged. She dismisses the musicians and asks her women for stories or news. It seems that Pothinus seeks an interview with Cleopatra and has bribed Ftatateeta to obtain it for him. The Queen says that she listens to the chatter of her women in order, as Caesar advised, to know them. Rebuking Ftatateeta, she sends for Pothinus.

Cleopatra paces to and fro, restless and angry while Iras wishes Caesar were in Rome and Charmian complains that he has made the Queen too serious. Pothinus enters and complains that he is a prisoner. Charmian warns him that Cleopatra is no longer a child, mockingly telling him he could also grow older and wiser in a day simply by being thrown from the lighthouse into the sea. Cleopatra sends the women out, but not before Ftatateeta has rebuked her for wanting to be a New Woman, the name given to women who struggled for women's rights in the 1890s and later.

Pothinus notices the change in her, which Cleopatra defines as a shift from foolishly doing what she likes to doing what must be done; this is not happiness, but greatness. Pothinus tells her he wishes to be freed, but Cleopatra knows that he had a different plan in mind which he has to abandon now that Cleopatra is no longer childish. Cleopatra tells him she will rule Egypt when Caesar has gone, as he surely will, for he does not love her. Caesar loves no one because he hates no one, being kind to people and animals alike. Nor does she love the god-like Caesar, but a more human and vulnerable Roman, whom Caesar has promised to send to her. She warns Pothinus that his plan to defeat Caesar and rule

Egypt by using Ptolemy as a puppet will not work. She goes out leaving Pothinus in a rage.

Ftatateeta enters, learning from Pothinus that he will resist Cleopatra to the death, and advises him to ask Lucius Septimius to plead with Cleopatra. But he goes out, hinting at another plan.

On the roof of the palace a table is set, for it is near dinner time. A 'majestic palace official' enters with Rufio. They climb the staircase, followed by a slave carrying a stool. Rufio sits down in the shade to await Caesar. Another official enters from the other side, walking backwards and announces Caesar's presence. Enter Caesar, freshly bathed, wearing a purple tunic and followed by two slaves with a couch. We learn that Caesar is pretending that it is his birthday for the purposes of entertaining Apollodorus! Rufio's contempt for this 'popinjay' is not shared by Caesar, who finds him amusing company and a rest from a life of action. Rufio wants a secret talk before dinner, so Caesar has the curtains drawn to reveal the bustling banquet preparations. No one will suspect now that they are discussing anything important. Rufio tells Caesar that he must see Pothinus, for the women are plotting something. Caesar, learning that Pothinus is the King's adviser and a prisoner, rebukes Rufio for not allowing his escape. Pothinus has stayed near Caesar to spy on him. Caesar decides to see him, and Pothinus, warning Caesar of danger, makes him an offer. His sly preamble leaves him time only to say that Cleopatra is a traitress, before the Queen appears beautifully dressed. Caesar now asks Pothinus to continue. He refuses, so Caesar declares that he is free to go. Pothinus blurts out that Cleopatra is using Caesar and will then either pack him off to Rome or have him killed. Cleopatra angrily protests, but Caesar tells her it is best to listen. He then tells Pothinus that he is foolish to be concerned about what is only natural. Caesar takes Pothinus inside, saying that he is not opposed to a reasonable settlement of the country's affairs, while Cleopatra hurriedly orders Ftatateeta to kill Pothinus, or never return.

Caesar comes back with Rufio and Apollodorus, who gracefully compliments Cleopatra on her womanly beauty. They go in to dine on sea food followed by peacocks' brains, nightingales' tongues and roast boar. Caesar is persuaded to take a little wine, and plans to find the source of the Nile and build a holy city there rather than return to Rome which bores him. Cleopatra loves this idea, and consults an effigy of the Sphinx as to a name for this new city. She hopes the god of the Nile will communicate by knocking on the table. They all repeat after her 'send us thy voice, Father Nile.' There is a terrifying cry of pain from off stage. Caesar wants to know what has happened; Cleopatra pretends it is the cry of a slave being beaten. Rufio's experience tells him it is a man being knifed, and Apollodorus hears a thud. We hear the noise of a crowd on the beach. Ftatateeta enters, strangely intoxicated. This confirms

Rufio's suspicions. Cleopatra embraces her nurse savagely and gives her many jewels. She meets Caesar's questions with denials that she has done anything. Rufio fears a riot with attempts to kill Caesar. Caesar accuses Cleopatra of deceit based on fear, but tells her she has not betrayed him since he has not trusted her. He is about to leave when Apollodorus and Britannus drag in Lucius Septimius followed by Rufio, who reports a riot in which Lucius was joining. Caesar, questioning Lucius, learns that the riot is about the death of Pothinus; he turns to rebuke Rufio, but Cleopatra declares that the man died by her order. She turns to Lucius, Apollodorus, and finally Britannus for support. They agree with her. Caesar is bitter, for he knows that vengeance leads to a chain of revenge.

Caesar tells Cleopatra that since she has renounced him, she must take the consequences of her doctrine of revenge and defend herself against attack. She pleads for protection as the sun begins to set. Caesar angrily calls them all fools who have been safe so far only because of his wisdom. He now enjoys telling them they will probably die like dogs in the streets. He prepares to meet his fate. The others want to live, and Lucius now says he will change sides to follow Caesar. He wants a command in the army in exchange for news. Caesar guesses rightly that Mithridates of Pergamos has come with reinforcements. Lucius admits this. Mithridates has captured Pelusium. Caesar accepts Lucius as an officer. The Egyptian forces under Achillas have gone to fight Mithridates, and only a mob roams the streets. Caesar immediately uses the dinner table to plan his escape from the city and a battle against Achillas. Half Caesar's forces will embark for the western lake while Caesar will march with the rest around the lake and up the Nile to join Mithridates. Caesar engages Apollodorus for the battle and the Romans in high-spirits make ready for action.

Cleopatra timidly asks whether Caesar has forgotten her, but Caesar, promising that on his return her affairs will be settled, goes off leaving her speechless with 'rage and humiliation'. Rufio tells her that if Pothinus's throat had been slit, he could not have cried out. Rufio pulls the curtains to the dining area, notices Ftatateeta at prayer, and asks Cleopatra if her nurse was Pothinus's killer. Cleopatra warns him that her enemies should beware of the woman who killed Pothinus. Rufio goes out easing his sword in its sheath. There are cries of 'Hail, Caesar!' from below. The bucina and several trumpets can be heard. Cleopatra, feeling lonely, calls Ftatateeta, but, getting no response, pulls open the curtains to discover Ftatateeta 'lying dead on the altar of Ra, with her throat cut. Her blood deluges the white stone.'

44 · Summaries

NOTES AND GLOSSARY:
boudoir: a lady's private sitting room often next to or including her bedroom
Pythagoras: Greek philosopher and mathematician in the sixth century BC
baldrick: a leather belt worn across the chest to carry a sword or horn
pommel: a knob on the end of a sword's handle
Jupiter Olympus: the chief Roman god, identified with the Greek god Zeus, and sometimes referred to as Jove
Lake Mareotis: a lake near Alexandria. The region is known for its wine
Fieldfares: a species of thrush
Falernian: from the region of Falernus in Campania; its wine was praised by Roman poets
table rapping: the knocking on the table around which people sit at a seance. Supposedly, spirits of the dead try to communicate by table rapping
Pelusiam (later Tineh): a defensive garrison town in Egypt, at the entrance to one of the mouths of the Nile

Act V

A festival and military display is taking place at noon in front of the palace. Caesar's gorgeously decorated galley can be seen alongside the quay. A Roman guard stands on the gangway to the esplanade. The steps to the central gate at the palace front are crowded with Cleopatra's ladies in their gayest clothes. Cleopatra's guards line the palace facade, while the north side of the esplanade is lined by Roman soldiers with townspeople behind them. Belzanor, the Persian and Centurion stroll among the other officers on the esplanade.

Apollodorus enters through the crowd and is allowed to pass through the line of soldiers to Belzanor, who asks him whether Caesar is nearby. Apollodorus reports that Caesar is still in the market place, having spared the lives of the Egyptian priests and purchased their gold and ivory god Apis; that King Ptolemy was drowned when his barge sank after the Romans had driven the Egyptians into the Nile; and that Caesar is a little delayed because 'he was settling the Jewish question.'

Trumpets announce the arrival of Caesar with Rufio and Britannus. Caesar asks Rufio what has to be done before his departure and discovers that he still has to appoint a Roman governor of Egypt. Rufio opposes Caesar's suggestion of Mithridates, reasoning that he will be needed for fighting their way back to Rome. Caesar appoints Rufio, squashing his protests with effective rhetoric. Caesar next desires to free his slave, but Britannus refuses, saying 'only as Caesar's slave have I found real freedom.' Caesar then leaves Apollodorus in charge of Egyptian art works, which he will send to Rome in exchange for what Caesar calls the arts of peace, war, government and civilisation. With this, Caesar makes his farewells, but feels he has forgotten something.

Cleopatra enters, dressed in black, without ornament or jewellery. She rebukes Caesar coldly for forgetting to say farewell to her. Bitterly ironic, she tells Caesar that the reason for her mourning is known to Rufio, the governor appointed to rule by Caesar's law of no punishment, revenge or judgments. Caesar approves this speech and Rufio agrees with its wisdom, but tells a parable of a hungry lion which Caesar would not punish, but merely 'kill it, without malice' to prevent it from killing him. Rufio claims he killed Ftatateeta in this spirit. Caesar praises Rufio, but Cleopatra is still angry about the death of her nurse. Caesar then promises to send her 'a beautiful present from Rome', Mark Antony. Caesar says farewell, boards his ship and waves to Rufio. Cleopatra, weeping, waves her handkerchief to Caesar as the ship moves and the soldiers draw their swords, crying 'Hail, Caesar!'

NOTES AND GLOSSARY:

Apis: ancient Egyptian god in the form of a sacred bull
Eupator: 'The Great.' Title given to Mithridates
Numidia: an ancient kingdom, then a Roman province, in Northern Africa
I shall have to buy it for you in Alexandria: Alexandria was a centre of commerce, trade and crafts
swop: exchange or trade one thing for another. The word is commonly used among schoolboys

Notes on Shaw's notes to *Caesar and Cleopatra*

Anachronism: a confusion of one historical period with another. Rum had not yet been invented during Cleopatra's lifetime
Galen: Greek medical man and anatomist (AD130?–201?)
Murray, Gilbert: English classical scholar and translator of Greek drama (1866–1957)
Hittites: ancient people of Asia Minor and northern Syria in the period about 2000–1200BC
Mauser rifle: an automatic weapon invented by Peter Paul Mauser (1838–1914), a German arms manufacturer
first syllable of recorded time: Shaw adapts Shakespeare's 'last syllable of recorded time' from Macbeth's world-weary speech in *Macbeth*, Act V Scene 5, line 21

46 · Summaries

Don Quixote and Sancho: the lean, fantastic hero and the fat villager who serves as his squire in Cervantes' book *Don Quixote*

Tamino and Papageno: characters in Wolfgang Amadeus Mozart's (1756–91) opera *The Magic Flute* (1791); the first one a serious hero, the second comic

Newton: Sir Isaac Newton (1642–1727) was an English mathematician and scientist whose Law of Gravitation dominated physics until Albert Einstein (1879–1955), the German physicist, worked out his relativity theory and changed our notion of the physical universe

Job: a man whose faith in God was tested but not broken by all kinds of hardships. The Book of Job tells his story in the Old Testament

Cicero: Marcus Tullius Cicero (106–43BC), Roman statesman and orator

Washington, George: (1732–1799) First President of the United States from 1789 to 1797

fin de siècle: (French) 'end of the century'; this phrase is used to refer to the period of 'decadence' at the end of the nineteenth century

the birds of Aristophanes: *The Birds*, a play by the Athenian comic and satirical playwright Aristophanes (448?–380?BC)

Socrates: Greek philosopher and teacher (470?–399BC) condemned to death on a charge of corrupting youth

Quince, Bottom: comic characters in Shakespeare's *A Midsummer Night's Dream*

Piraeus: major seaport of Greece, near Athens

Glaucon and Polemarchus: Glaucon was a writer of dialogues in ancient Athens. Polemarchus was the assassin of Ploydorus, a King of Sparta

Kephalus or Cephalus: an orator in Plato's *Republic*, Cephalus was father of Polemarchus

Mr Podsnap: a pompous, moralistic character in *Our Mutual Friend* (1864–65) a novel by the English writer Charles Dickens (1812–1870)

the style is the man: a saying of Comte Georges de Buffon (1707–88), a French writer and naturalist

Darwin, Charles Robert: English naturalist (1809–82) who, in his *On the Origin of Species* (1859) set out the theory of evolution by natural selection

Charles XII: King of Sweden (1682–1718) and one of the most intelligent generals of this period

Nelson:	Horatio Nelson (1758–1805) was the great English admiral who won the Battle of Trafalgar, in which he was killed, but which helped to defeat Napoleon. Nelson's memorial column stands in Trafalgar Square, London
Joan of Arc:	the French Saint, heroine and military leader (1412–1431) who was condemned as a witch and heretic to be burnt at the stake
Gladstone:	William Ewart Gladstone (1809–1898) English statesman and four times Prime Minister
Treasury bench:	seats on the Government's side of the House of Commons occupied by the Chancellor of the Exchequer
Columbus:	the Italian navigator, Cristoforo Colombo (1451–1506), who, working for Spain, opened up America to western explorers
Franklin:	Sir John Franklin (1786–1847) English explorer of the Arctic

Part 3

Commentary

Nature and purpose of the work

Caesar and Cleopatra was first printed in *Three Plays for Puritans*. It was a puritan work in the sense that Shaw made Caesar's role not that of the lover but the statesman-soldier; the play thus rejected that theatre of sexual love, with its coyness and moral dishonesty, which delighted audiences at the time. Shaw explained his point of view in his Preface. Moreover, by not following Shakespeare's *Antony and Cleopatra* (1606–7) and the adaptation of it, *All for Love* (1677) by the English dramatist John Dryden (1631–1700), Shaw at once gained some originality and avoided the trap of trying to compete with these two major tragedies.

Shaw's play was subtitled 'A History'; it was a history play not merely because it was set in the past but because the role of Caesar, Shaw claimed, was based on the views of one of the best historians of the period, Theodor Mommsen. Shaw departed from the Caesar of Shakespeare's *Julius Caesar* (1599) presenting instead a comedian, an even-tempered, anti-heroic man who relies on reason, intelligence and a shrewd eye for people (see discussion of characters below, pp. 52–3).

Shaw's use of the history play form is full of humour. The smuggling of Cleopatra to the lighthouse in a carpet is a piece of comic action. But Shaw also enjoys comedy arising from language. The characters do not speak in some noble style we might imagine to be fitting for a Roman or an ancient Egyptian; their talk is based on the modern speech of Shaw's England. Apollodorus speaks with the tones of a snobbish, rather pretentious collector of art. We know he is an 'aesthete' of the 1890s. Shaw can make fun of him for example, by contrasting him and his speech with the common sense of Caesar:

> APOLLODORUS: Friend Rufio threw a pearl into the sea: Caesar fished up a diamond.
> CAESAR: Caesar fished up a touch of rheumatism, my friend.

The name of Cleopatra's nurse might well have been difficult for a Roman to pronounce, but Shaw makes comedy from the name in a way thoroughly English. Caesar gives her nicknames easier to pronounce.

FTATATEETA: Who pronounces the name of Ftatateeta, the Queen's chief nurse?
CAESAR: Nobody can pronounce it, Tota, except yourself.

When Caesar and Pothinus are negotiating in Act IV, Caesar and Rufio talk as if they are a pair of modern English comedians:

POTHINUS: Caesar: I come to warn you of a danger, and to make you an offer.
CAESAR: Never mind the danger. Make the offer.
RUFIO: Never mind the offer. What's the danger?

Cleopatra makes fun of Caesar's baldness at the end of Act III and of Britannus's Englishness when she questions him about woad. Britannus reacts like a Victorian Englishman.

This humorous approach and the modern speech and modern attitudes in the play show that the author is using the historical setting and characters for his own purposes. He is not trying to reconstruct the past in realistic detail, although many of his details are historically correct. He is assuming that human nature is much the same as it was in the time of Caesar and that the arts of war and peace and good government have changed very little from the point of view of human motives. The British Empire had a profit motive, just as Caesar's purpose in Egypt was to raise taxes. Shaw's Caesar tries to teach Cleopatra leadership and good government. Shaw at the same time is trying to teach the same lessons to the officials of the British Empire. Shaw's Ireland was at the time (like Egypt to Caesar) a British possession. Modern Egypt was also under British control.

Shaw was also teaching the women in his audience about politics. Women in England were struggling to get the right to vote in general elections. Cleopatra progresses from a girl with no political sense to a queen who starts to make her own decisions. Shaw shows that Cleopatra could think politically, although she does not fully absorb Caesar's wisdom. She risks her own and Caesar's life and rule when she has Pothinus killed. She prefers Antony as a lover to Caesar as a mentor.

Caesar, in teaching these lessons, becomes in some ways a self-portrait of Shaw, who influenced English society through his teachings in his writing, his Fabianism, his work as a vestryman and his numerous speeches. On the other hand Caesar is unlike Shaw because he does not care about the arts of literature, music and painting. Besides, Caesar controls an Empire. Shaw also showed that Caesar was in some ways less than successful. His campaign in Egypt, Shaw suggests, is largely a matter of hasty improvisation rather than brilliant strategy.

The prologue speech of Ra does more than give the audience necessary background information (the *exposition* of the play) about

Caesar's Egyptian campaign and his struggle with Pompey. It also presents Caesar as a modern politician ('he bought men with words and with gold, even as ye are bought') It stresses the way history will be seen as just like modern times, and modern men will be just as foolish as those in past times. The god Ra sees everything from the viewpoint of eternity, and this is the vision, too, of Shaw the satirist:

> RA: Ye poor posterity, think not that ye are the first. Other fools before ye have seen the sun rise and set, and the moon change her shape and her hour. As they were so ye are; and yet not so great; for the pyramids my people built stand to this day; whilst the dustheaps on which ye slave, and which ye call empires, scatter in the wind even as ye pile your dead sons' bodies on them to make yet more dust.

The lofty style of Ra's speech contrasts with the colloquial speech of the play itself, just as gods are loftier than men, and the civilisation which produced the Valley of the Kings, the pyramids and the Sphinx is to him greater than that of the Romans and their successors, the British.

The characters

Shaw's stage directions supply full instructions for stage settings and atmosphere, and give many statements about the characters. His intentions about his characters are clear. Characterisation (the way an author builds up his characters) is also achieved most effectively, of course, through what the characters actually do, what they say, *and* what is said about them. But how they are acted is another major factor. Characters are also *roles* for actors. An actor playing Caesar must present him as wise, clever, human and on the whole sympathetic. The actress playing Cleopatra must be a girlish and adolescent child who progresses and changes (as young people usually do) to become shrewder. She must become a lovely young woman more aware of herself as a queen, but still having human weaknesses. If Cleopatra is played as too silly and kittenish we lose interest in whether Caesar can teach her anything. If she were played as serious and not very childish at the start of the play, the role would again mar the effect of the play. Cleopatra *must* be girlish and spontaneous, and she *must* change as the play progresses. Having thought about *role*, it is well to remember the main features of the characters themselves, given here in the order of their appearance in the play.

Ra

Ra is the ancient Egyptian god who speaks the Prologue of the play. He must be awesome and mysterious. He wears a hawk's head mask. His tone is one of contempt for the audience. Human beings are the objects of his satire, being petty and sinful. His speech is elevated and archaic in style; it gives the impression of a timeless being who sees the folly of mankind at all times. The voice, acting, costuming and lighting of Ra are all vital to the effectiveness of the Prologue speech.

Belzanor

'Belzanor is a typical veteran, tough and wilful; prompt, capable and crafty where brute force will serve; helpless and boyish when it will not': thus Shaw sums him up. Although Shaw tells us he would be a first rate Sergeant, he gives him the rank of Captain in the play, thus making him an officer. Belzanor is suspicious of the Persian because he is a foreigner; he does not enjoy losing his game of dice to the Persian. Like the other palace guards, he believes himself descended from a god. He has a keen sense of his own importance, courage and dignity. His pride and sense of honour are thoroughly Egyptian, so that he cannot understand the Romans who 'fight to win,' as the more realistic Bel Affris tells him. Belzanor is an old soldier, fifty years of age, but he is superstitious. Like the Persian and Bel Affris, he appears in the Alternative to the Prologue for the purposes of exposition, or giving the audience basic information on which dramatic situations are built.

The Persian

A sly young man, the Persian is quick-thinking and knows the ways of the world. He is pleased with his cleverness. He reveals a cold and merciless character in his plans to seize Cleopatra, sell her to Ptolemy, her brother and rival for the throne, and allow the Romans to slaughter captive women in order to save ransom money. He is cunning and murderous: only Ftatateeta's own quick action saves her from his knife. His questions in Act V draw out information which helps to bring the plot to its resolution, preparing for the final appearance of Caesar.

Bel Affris

A young officer, proud of his wounds, 'a fairhaired dandy' of noble birth, Bel Affris has the role of a messenger. He tells us of the Roman tactics in battle. He is a realist, unafraid of death, and gives the impression that Romans are merciless. His speeches give the exposition, preparing for the first appearance of Caesar. The costume, coolheadedness and interesting information of Bel Affris make this role able to hold the audience's attention. It is a small part, but it serves the purpose of building up our expectations.

Ftatateeta

She is Cleopatra's nurse. Immensely strong and evil-tempered, she is vividly described by Shaw as having a wrinkled face 'with the mouth of a bloodhound and the jaws of a bulldog'. She is proud and cunning. She dominates all except Caesar and, later, Cleopatra. On orders from Cleopatra, she kills Pothinus. Satisfied by shedding blood, she carries out the rituals of her religion. She is savage, yet at heart a servant, and the masterful Caesar shows Cleopatra how to control Ftatateeta. The old nurse is faithful to her mistress to the end. The role offers good theatrical opportunities for comic and other stage business. Consider, for instance, her scuffles with the sentinel in Act III.

Caesar

Presented by Shaw as fifty-four years old, bald and a wise ruler, Caesar is the unheroic hero of the play. Caesar's monologue at his first entry reveals a thoughtful man who identifies himself unconvincingly with the Sphinx, a symbol of inscrutable wisdom. Some sense of Caesar's power is achieved but his humanity is also emphasised by means of contrast with Cleopatra's girlish and superstitious view of him: 'His father was a tiger and his mother a burning mountain; and his nose is like an elephant's trunk.' Caesar is, in fact, fatherly, full of common sense, practical and intelligent.

Caesar reveals his sense of humour in his teasing of Cleopatra. He spends much of his time teaching her to be a ruler, thus revealing by his own actions and ideas the qualities of the leader. He encourages her in Act I to be brave, commanding and yet merciful. In Act II, he demonstrates these qualities himself; he is calm when he hears of the Egyptian army's advance; he shows mercy to Lucius Septimius, the Roman who beheaded Pompey; he preserves his authority even when facing possible defeat. He also shows tact, restraint and kindness when he listens to Cleopatra cheekily telling him he should learn from her. His mercy is not weakness or foolishness.

Caesar is very practical. He needs as much support as he can get. He responds to necessity. To take Egyptian prisoners would require twice as many Roman soldiers merely to guard them. Caesar prefers to use them in battle. He defends his position by cunning and manipulation. He diverts Achillas's hostile legions by suggesting to the panicky Theodotus that they could help save the library by helping the firefighters.

Caesar appears light-hearted yet shrewd. He is daring when he leaps into the sea to escape the Egyptians in Act III. In Act IV, Cleopatra sums up Caesar's kindness, distinguishing it from love. Caesar reveals the puritanical side of his nature when he comments on the rose-leaf cushions and the expensive seafood prepared for his birthday feast. He refers to religious ritual as 'hocus-pocus'. Caesar is blunt but also willing to face reality himself. He thinks it only natural that Cleopatra should want to be rid of his dominion over her and Egypt. He accepts her attitude as inevitable. He is reasonable in his willingness to negotiate with Pothinus. He is human in that he does not realise Cleopatra has ordered Pothinus's death. Caesar is wise in that he treats Rufio not as a slave but as another human being; he values Rufio's opinions and truths even though Rufio is sometimes argumentative. Caesar also demonstrates extraordinary calm in the face of death. He is also quick thinking. When Lucius changes sides to support him, Caesar quickly deduces that his reinforcements led by Mithridates are at hand. He immediately improvises a bold battle plan. Here is Caesar the general and veteran of many successful campaigns.

In Act V Caesar shows himself once more to be an efficient ruler and administrator. He is level-headed and can contemplate calmly his possible death when he returns to Rome. Caesar surprises Cleopatra once more by excusing the killing of Ftatateeta by saying Rufio did it not out of revenge, punishment or judgment, but out of necessity, as one would kill a dangerous lion. He shows his knowledge of the human heart and his 'fatherly' affection when he promises to send Mark Antony to Cleopatra. It is a rich and demanding part with many sides to it. It requires an actor of great range, serious and comic, colloquial and rhetorical, nobly heroic, yet human and unheroic.

Cleopatra

Cleopatra contrasts vividly with Caesar. She is immature; unlike Caesar, she changes during the course of the play. At first she is a superstitious girl of sixteen, afraid of her nurse, afraid of the Romans and afraid of Caesar. In Act I she heeds Caesar's first lesson: do not show fear. Her impulsive, childish behaviour towards her servants shows that she has much to learn yet before she can become a queen. She has to learn not only courage, but pride and majesty to dignify her beauty. By the end of Act I Shaw has given us a Cleopatra who is girlish, warm-hearted, cruel, superstitious, eager to learn, weak, frightened, gaily impulsive, honest, foolish, rapturous: in short, a volatile adolescent whom Caesar hopes to turn into a queen. Caesar's humbling of Ftatateeta demonstrates for Cleopatra how a ruler's force of personal authority and power to give orders can be used to control others. At this stage, Cleopatra sees only how quickly she can throw off her nurse's old rule over her. She does not yet know how to behave like a queen nor how to use her power.

In Act II, Ftatateeta enters as if she were a queen. Cleopatra is still the girl hiding behind her nurse. But she questions Caesar about his conversation with the mutinous Achillas and Pothinus, puzzled that Caesar listens calmly. He explains that they are speaking the truth. Cleopatra watches Caesar's behaviour and then threatens to throw Ftatateeta to the crocodiles. Her youthful arrogance is at its worst when she tells Caesar, 'If you do as I tell you, you will soon learn to govern.' She shows, too, that she does not yet know that Caesar must work: power has its duties. At a time of battle, Cleopatra merely teases Caesar about his baldness.

Act III shows Cleopatra's new command over Ftatateeta firmly established: she even orders the nurse to strangle the sentinel, an order which points to the murder of Pothinus in Act V. Though her power and courage are growing, she is still silly and thoughtless, as the carpet trick reveals. Caesar shows her that one soldier's hand is worth more in battle than her head. She learns that Caesar will not play with her, or be a lover. He will not show her illusions. To stay near Caesar, she must become more realistic. When she is thrown into the sea, fun turns into a struggle to survive. During the six months which pass between Act III and Act IV, Cleopatra has learned a good deal. In her dealings with the musician, she shows that she can judge for herself: she knows a fraud when she sees one. Her scene with her court ladies shows that she has learned from Caesar how to listen to people in order to know them. She is now totally in command of Ftatateeta. Her talk with Pothinus shows her to be the Queen: she is dignified, intelligent and tries to follow Caesar's example. She tells Pothinus 'Now that Caesar has made me wise, it is no use my liking or disliking: I do what must be done . . . If Caesar were gone, I think I could govern the Egyptians; for what Caesar is to me, I am to the fools around me.' Now she has confidence. Now she is talking like a ruler. She has become a woman. Yet she has more to learn from Caesar. She is so angry when Pothinus says she is a traitor to Caesar, that she orders Pothinus's death. This shows that she has not yet learnt how to use power or be merciful. Caesar knows how to use mercy for his own good. She does not. Her hasty action almost brings about Caesar's defeat. She still needs his cleverness and foresight.

In Act V Cleopatra appears in mourning for Ftatateeta. She is angered greatly by her death at Rufio's hands. Caesar's final lesson is that sometimes in order to govern one has to kill. But it must be done only out of necessity, not malice. If Cleopatra has not yet learned how to govern, at least she is made to realise the force of Caesar's rules of government, 'without punishment. Without revenge. Without judgment.' She is now ready to learn how to love a man. Caesar leaves, promising to send her Mark Antony.

Pothinus

Like Caesar, Pothinus is a vigorous man of fifty. He is guardian to Ptolemy, being in this also like Caesar, who becomes a sort of guardian to Cleopatra. But unlike Caesar, Pothinus is of 'common mind and character; impatient and unable to control his temper'. He is thus when he appears a good foil to Caesar. He tries to resist Caesar's influence in Egypt but is no match for him as a leader or a teacher of statesmanship. Instead of teaching Ptolemy to think, as Caesar does with Cleopatra, he merely uses Ptolemy as an inadequate mouthpiece. Pothinus can also be paired with Ftatateeta, since he is a eunuch inferior in rank to his master the King. He rules Ptolemy just as Ftatateeta, at least at the start of the play, rules Cleopatra. Pothinus thinks of himself as wise and shrewd, but in his encounters with Caesar and, in Act IV, with Cleopatra, he always loses. Murdered by Ftatateeta, he fittingly is the cause of her death at Rufio's hands. He can be played as pompous, in contrast to Caesar's humour and depth.

Theodotus

Ptolemy's tutor is a minor comic part: a small, wrinkled, bird-like man, he is full of a sense of his own importance and wisdom. He has a squeaky voice. He could be an unkind satirical portrait of H. G. Wells whom Shaw met and disputed with in the Fabian society. Again, like Pothinus, he contrasts with Caesar in that he teaches a monarch, and becomes the butt of Caesar's irony when Caesar tells him: 'You teach men to be kings, Theodotus. That is very clever of you.' This fussy old teacher does not realise that there is more to life than books. But his genuine concern over the burning of the library gives another dimension to this minor role.

Ptolemy

The King of Egypt, brother and husband of Cleopatra, Ptolemy is a ten-year-old boy, whom Shaw presents as a 'mixture of impotence and petulance'. He is young enough and childish enough to be bullied by Cleopatra, and is totally in the control of his guardian and tutor, who try to rule through him. He is clearly nervous and inadequate for his position. He is unable to understand politics enough even to question the fact that there are Romans in Egypt. Caesar is kind to him knowing that he is only an unhappy little boy who usually has to be on his best behaviour.

Achillas

He is the general in charge of Ptolemy's army and says he was left as commander of the Roman forces in Egypt when Antony had put Cleopatra's father on the throne. He is dominated by Caesar. He tries to appear forceful: 'I am the Roman general here, Caesar.' But Caesar is merely amused by his trying to be both Roman and Egyptian. This small part, confined to Act II, serves just to establish that there is an Egyptian army which outnumbers Caesar's meagre forces.

Rufio

He is a rough but honest soldier, a competent professional officer. He is practical, courageous and, though bold and frank in his criticism of Caesar, is a good student of Caesar's methods. His killing of Ftatateeta, once he sees the need for it, is prompt. Caesar, because he can trust Rufio, leaves him to govern Egypt at the end of the play.

Britannus

Stiff, rather formal and sometimes proud, Caesar's secretary is supposed to be an ancient Briton. He is actually a late Victorian Englishman meant by Shaw to suggest some Victorian attitudes common in English society. He is proud to be British. He has clean moral attitudes, being shocked by the ancient custom of marriage between royal brothers and sisters. He is quick to remind Caesar of his duty to Rome when Caesar spares Lucius Septimius, killer of Pompey. He tries to preserve Caesar's dignity, as when he scolds Cleopatra for teasing Caesar about his baldness. He distrusts Apollodorus, thinking he is a professional artist. He accepts Apollodorus when he learns that he is a nobleman who is an amateur artist. This suggests English distrust of both art and professionalism. He has a haughty attitude to strangers, feeling that his official position gives him authority. Shaw's satirical portrait of an Englishman stresses his respectability. When Britannus explains that Britons paint themselves blue to prevent their dead being left naked on the battle field, Shaw's satire on British ideas of respectability becomes gaily anti-Victorian. Shaw's satire of the British sense of honour and revenge is more serious when Caesar says 'I do not make human sacrifices to my honor, as your Druids do.'

Lucius Septimius

An experienced campaigner, he has beheaded Pompey. He is a careful opportunist, hoping to be favoured by Caesar. When he thinks the

Egyptians are likely to defeat Caesar in Act II, he joins them. It is Lucius who, in Act IV, brings news of Pothinus's death, and knowing of the reinforcements Mithridates brings to Caesar, again switches sides. He thus survives by supporting Caesar.

The Sentinel

This character is representative of the common man, the ordinary soldier in a garrison. By delaying the escape of Cleopatra from the Palace, he is doing his duty, and at the same time serves to create some tension, suspense and stage action. His dutiful, rough and totally inartistic nature serves to contrast with the flamboyant Apollodorus. It is a good minor comic role.

Apollodorus

Literally his name means Golden Apollo (Apollo was the Greek god of the arts). He is the Roman equivalent of the rich young dandies of London in the 1890s. He is an aesthete. He loves art. He thinks art has no purpose but to be beautiful. It is its own reward. This is the doctrine of Art for Art's sake, which Shaw humorously makes the Sentinel ignorantly take to be a guess at the password. Apollodorus, 'handsome and debonair', is also clever. He brings a satirical element, full of colour, gaiety and fun to the play.

His remarks are sometimes pretentious, and his compliments fulsome, as when he speaks to Cleopatra, but he also has a gift for epigrams: 'Majesty: when a stupid man is doing something he is ashamed of, he always declares that it is his duty.' He lives life as if it were art, and would prefer to die beautifully than by some ugly means. He is thus able to sport with his life, and it is he who makes the impulsive and daring gesture by diving into the sea. This shows Caesar how he can escape the enemy army. He plays at being Cleopatra's 'faithful knight' but there is no sign that he really loves her. Clearly, he will be no match for Mark Antony. He is, in sum, a part invented mainly as a plot mechanism, but he is a glittering and amusing one.

Charmian and Iras

These are Cleopatra's court companions. Like the musicians, they are minor characters serving to make Cleopatra seem wiser and more regal after her escape from the lighthouse.

Structure, theme and style

The structure of *Caesar and Cleopatra* is fairly simple. It is similar to that of many history plays, being episodic. The action starts in October 48BC and each scene follows in a chronological sequence from Act I. There is no jumping backward and forward in time so far as the events of the play are concerned. This episodic structure is modified, though, in two ways. There is a gap of six months between Acts III and IV. This makes Cleopatra's change and growth as a person seem more likely. Second, the Prologue device introduces the play's action by giving us background information as part of the exposition. The Prologue of Ra is a soliloquy (a speech spoken by a character alone on the stage). It gives us a satirical way of looking at the play which follows. The alternative to the Prologue is a scene which again gives us exposition. It also gives us the human perspective on the events which follow: the panic the Romans cause and the difference between the older world of the Egyptians and the modern world of the Romans. Both Prologues make the point that the history play is a mirror of the modern world.

The plot of *Caesar and Cleopatra* follows this simple, episodic structure over five acts. Act I has three main sections: Caesar's speech to the Sphinx; the meeting of Caesar and Cleopatra, giving us the differences between them, and the way they are attracted to each other; finally, the establishment of Cleopatra as queen. The climax of Act I is Cleopatra's discovery that her 'old gentleman' is in fact Caesar. Cleopatra's illusions and superstitions are contrasted with the mature reality of Caesar. The smashing of illusions is one of Shaw's constant themes. Caesar educates Cleopatra by replacing illusions with examples of his realistic kind of behaviour during the remaining acts.

Act II has four main sections of action. The first has the entry of Ptolemy as King. Shaw contrasts the boy (who can only repeat things unconvincingly, and thus is not a ruler) with Cleopatra, who is learning to act on her own. The second section introduces the Roman characters more fully, contrasting them with the Egyptians. It shows how money is a basic motive in politics and war. It also shows how Caesar has the 'right' to be there only because of military power. The scene is full of political satire. It also reveals Caesar's compassion and his policy of mercy and peace-making after conflict. The third section shows Cleopatra's conversation with Caesar. She has already gained confidence from Caesar's friendship. It also shows her longing for Mark Antony. Cleopatra wants to be grown-up. The last section of the act deals with the approach of Achillas and his army. Caesar is a calm and efficient organiser. He contemplates destruction, even of a culture, with little regret: it leaves the way open for new construction. Shaw's theme is the heavy responsibility rulers have for the direction of society. They have to learn to watch battles, see things destroyed and be prepared to die themselves.

In this act Caesar seems very much in control. He is feared. Then there comes the reversal of the situation. The act has the spectacle of the fire (opportunity for lighting effects) and a climax of military action where Caesar faces defeat. Reversal and conflicts (Romans v. Egyptians; Cleopatra v. Ptolemy; Caesar v. his companions) make this a very lively piece of dramatic writing. In this act Caesar demonstrates his qualities as a ruler. Secondary themes emerge too: the satire of learning in the old pedant, Theodotus; the limitations of Nationalism ('Egypt for the Egyptians') which will not necessarily bring sound government; and the satire through Britannus of attitudes which assumed that British customs were the norm, the measure of all else.

Act III adds broad comedy to the satire. Its first part introduces a new interest, Apollodorus, and a new target of satire—aestheticism. It also shows the comic trick to get Cleopatra to the lighthouse. It continues the conflict between the Romans and Egyptians which persists throughout this act.

The scene at the lighthouse reveals to Cleopatra her most difficult truth: that she is not personally indispensable. The good ruler's duty to his followers is more important than his personal feeling. The good ruler knows that there are forces greater than any single human being, whatever his power and position. Caesar almost demonstrates that even he can be defeated, but by the leap into the sea he and his friends avoid capture. Cleopatra's lesson about her own personal unimportance is rudely demonstrated to her when she is thrown into the sea. The wetting of Cleopatra is a symbol, like Christian baptism. She is 'baptised' into the life of a ruler. Act III is less dramatic than Act II, but it is enlivened by theatrical effects such as the struggle with the sentries, the hauling of the carpet and the leap into the sea. These effects can work well in the theatre.

Through Britannus, Shaw again satirises nineteenth century England. By supposing the British invention of the steam engine to have existed in 48BC, Shaw implies that man's ingenuity has not really increased.

Although the themes are serious, the military position of the Romans very serious, and Caesar's personal fortunes very low, Act III is lighthearted in mood. The act ends in a climax of fun, with Britannus, who could face death, cheering like a schoolboy.

Act IV has two main sections: in the first we find Cleopatra dominating her servants, her court and Pothinus. She has been changed by her 'baptism' in the sea of politics and war, and by six months in Caesar's company. She is older, shrewder and willing to use her power politically, as with her misguided order for the murder of Pothinus. Cleopatra has grown, but she has not reached Caesar's level.

Caesar dominates the second part of the act. Whereas Cleopatra failed to secure the support of Pothinus, Caesar successfully responds to him and his revelation of Cleopatra's ambition to be rid of Caesar. He sets Pothinus free in order to work for a negotiated settlement. Caesar shows that he is a clever diplomat. His comments to Apollodorus add to Shaw's picture of Caesar as a comedian.

Act IV uses ritual effectively. The lighting for a rich sunset, the use of incense and the air of superstition create a sense of mystery in the action with the tripod before the statue of Ra. The sudden cry of a man offstage sounds like the cry of a spirit. Caesar knows that it is real not supernatural. Only Cleopatra knows at the time that it is Pothinus's death cry. At the same time, the scene suggests that it is Ra, the god, who really dominates events. Not even Caesar can prevent Pothinus's death.

Caesar, in fact, knows men. He also understands their limits. He is not deceived by Rome's imperial ambitions. He is not deceived by the need for revenge. Unlike Cleopatra, he knows that the killing of Pothinus can only lead to more bloodshed. Blood feud is an endless chain of killing. In his greatest speech, Caesar shows Cleopatra that she has made a serious mistake:

> And so, to the end of history, murder shall breed murder, always in the name of right and honor and peace, until the gods are tired of blood and create a race that can understand.

He teaches her his most terrible lesson, that those who take to themselves the power of life and death always themselves face death. Shaw gives us Cleopatra's weakness, and Caesar's strength, her folly and his wisdom, in the midst of seige. It is the most dramatic moment and the climax of the entire play, for Caesar is on the point of death at the hands of the mob. Shaw finishes the act with a swift reversal when Lucius joins Caesar and we learn of the arrival of reinforcements. This, too, seems like an act of the god Ra who watches the play like Fate itself. Our final vision is of Ftatateeta dead on the altar of Ra, as if she is the sacrifice which has spared Cleopatra and Caesar from destruction.

If Act IV was the climax of the entire play, Act V is its resolution. We learn all we need for Shaw to bring the action to a point of rest. The act must be short and swift. The preparations for Caesar's departure for Rome give a mood of festivity. This contrasts with the sombre deaths of Act IV. Shaw resolves the relationship between Caesar and Cleopatra by making Caesar regain some of his kindness towards her. Cleopatra's anger over the killing of Ftatateeta cannot be reduced by teaching her why Rufio killed her. Caesar has another answer. He promises to send Mark Antony. Cleopatra is now his friend again, full of joy. But her wisdom is still limited, as Rufio points out, when she follows her instincts in preferring Mark Antony to Caesar. Thus the themes of growth and teaching are raised again as the play comes to an end.

Shaw's dramatic style in the play is mainly satiric and comic, save for the darker moments in Act IV. Delight in word-play and a clever use of colloquial speech are typical. Ra's monologue is an experiment in speech suitable for a god, but its frequent use of biblical archaism is a cliché and not always convincing. Careful acting and staging could make it effective.

The imagery of the play affords great contrasts. The visual images of the setting in ancient Egypt are impressive, spectacular and exotic. They are romantic, and belong to the nineteenth century theatre. In contrast to these romantic and sometimes mysterious images, the dialogue is that of modern men and women. The imagery of the dialogue is on the whole deliberately commonplace and there is not much of it. There are, though, vivid symbolic images: Caesar is likened to the Sphinx; Cleopatra is symbolically thrown into the sea, the 'baptism' testing her survival into a new, adult life; and Ftatateeta becomes an image of blood sacrifice on the altar of Ra.

Part 4

Hints for study

Points to select for detailed study

Theme

The main theme of the play is the art of government. This is related to the relationship between Caesar and Cleopatra by the themes of teaching and growth. Related themes are the struggle for power and the uses of power, wise and foolish; the use of reason; the need for clemency; the use of force; the need to do what is necessary; duty and obligations to one's followers; the education of women.

Read the play, noting which themes emerge in each act. Select brief quotations or incidents which illustrate each theme. Make notes by writing brief headings (for example: *Need for clemency*) and under each heading list your examples, commenting on them to explain their function in the play.

Character

The characters are the heart of the play, for it is through their relationships, actions and personalities that the play develops and themes emerge. If we lose interest in characters, then we do not care what happens to them or what they think, and the play as a whole fails to impress us.

After you have read the play, read the notes on characters in Part 3. Make your own notes for each major character under the following headings:

Main character traits: is the character clever, foolish, friendly, mean, cruel, kind?

Actions done by the character: list only the main actions, noting where they occur in the play.

Associates: here list other characters with whom the character you are studying is involved. What is the nature of their involvement? Why are they linked to each other? What do other characters say or think about the character you are studying? Do characters form pairs or groups? If so, why are they so grouped?

Role: what kind of acting part is this character? Appearance, movement, general manner, habits, mode of speech may be useful things to notice here. Read the play looking for hints about the way the part could be acted. Does it give the actor good opportunities for comedy, for stage business, for emotional scenes? Be specific. Give examples. Does the role have a big scene or important speech? Remember that a minor character can be a good role for the actor. Are there any difficulties in the role?

All your notes should be brief and have short quotations or page references to illustrate your major points.

Setting

Your general reading of the play will have shown that the main setting in time and place is Egypt, 48–47BC. Put this down under the head of *Main setting*. Now ask yourself why the playwright chose that setting. Is it necessary for historical purposes? Is it symbolic of anything? Does distance from us in time and space help us to see the issues of the play more clearly? Does the setting add to our enjoyment of the play?

Now make a heading for each new scene, starting with the Prologue. Give *brief* details of the stage setting, including the kind of light indicated and any sound effects. In each case ask: What mood is created? Why? Is the setting visually impressive? Is it complicated or simple? Why? Are there ways in which the setting affects characters, reflects themes or aids stage action? If so, in what ways?

Stage action, conflict, crisis

All drama presents actions involving conflict or struggle before an audience. If the drama is to maintain interest there must be a doubt or problem about the result of the conflict. This creates suspense. The author will maintain the suspense by keeping us wanting to know either (a) What will happen or (b) How it will happen or, perhaps, both. He achieves this by means of arranging the action of the play so as to produce conflicts and crises. A crisis is a moment of action which has more emotional excitement than other moments and leaves us wondering what will happen next. It may be a moment of great joy or despair, or victory or defeat; it may result from a sudden revelation, as when Cleopatra learns that she is of no use to Caesar at the lighthouse; or from a reversal bringing misfortune or uncertainty. The climax of the play is the greatest crisis of all. It is usually near the end of the play, so that the release of tension after the climax may provide a short period to resolve loose strands in the plot before the end of the play.

Internal and external drama

Dramatic actions, conflicts and crises may be *internal* (within a character's own mind, as when he has to reach a moment of decision) or *external* (between two or more characters). Remember that external actions may be accomplished through speeches, dialogue and expressions of ideas, thoughts, desires *as well as through physical actions*. In most good drama, as well as in Shaw's plays, dramatic effects are obtained mainly through what characters say. Physical actions on the stage, such as fights, are used to show conflict, and at moments of crisis or climax, but they are less frequent than dramatic actions, conflicts and crises achieved through dialogue. They are effects of theatre and spectacle. If physical action is put in a scene merely for the fun or thrills of it, then it is merely spectacle. If it arises naturally from the interplay of characters, the clash of wills and personalities, then it is also dramatic.

Segments of action

Plays, from beginning to end, show segments of action to the audience. Each segment will achieve something. A series of these segments will form a scene or act. In Act I, the first segment of action is the entry of Caesar described in the stage directions. This segment achieves the following: (a) It gets Caesar on stage. (b) It establishes *through his manner* that he is contemplative, stealthy and full of wonder at his surroundings. His movement must therefore be expressive of this state of mind. (c) It establishes a scale by which the human Caesar seems small and overshadowed by the colossal works of the past. This is achieved by the setting. (d) It prepares us for the next segment, Caesar's monologue to the Sphinx.

If the next segment of Act I is the address to the Sphinx, segment three is the conversation between Cleopatra and Caesar up to the point where 'they steal across the desert' to the palace.

Each segment of action usually begins when a new event occurs, a new character appears, or where there is a decisive shift of mood or action. By dividing each act into its segments of action we can see clearly what each adds to the play, what its mood is, whether its purpose is characterisation, conflict or crisis.

Under the heading of *action, conflict, crisis* make a list of segments of action in each act of the play. Give each segment a number and title (For instance, under Act 1. 3, 'Cleopatra's first talk with Caesar'). Under this put *Aim* and note the purpose of the segment. Then note beneath these the dominant *mood* or *moods*. Is it comic? Light-hearted? Is it one of amazement?

Conflict, crisis, recognition, reversal will be useful headings if there is anything in the segment appropriate to them. If there is not, leave them out of your list. Under *plot* and *character* briefly write down any new development worth noticing.

Having completed this for each act, you will be able to see what the main actions, conflicts and crises are and where they appear in the play. You may notice patterns. Cleopatra's girlhood in the play begins with her surprising Caesar at the Sphinx. It ends when she surprises him at the lighthouse.

Language

Unless it is expressed in pure mime, drama uses words. The dramatist tries to give his play language appropriate to it. He tries to make his characters speak convincing dialogue so that we seem to be overhearing the real speech of the characters. He tries to give each character a style of speech appropriate to that character alone. Thus Britannus does not speak in exactly the same way as Ftatateeta. Apollodorus's speech is different again. *Make notes describing the kind of speech used by each of these characters.*

Good plays, though, use language also to reinforce themes and moods. The kind of words used (*diction*) and the use of figurative language, such as simile and metaphor (*imagery*) may be important.

Read through the play noting the *frequency* and the *purpose* of references to the following significant words and images: the cat, the gods, water, the Sphinx, the serpent, blood, spears, the desert, Rome, the bucina, the lighthouse. Make notes on the diction of the play to show how certain words suggest the ancient worlds of Rome and Egypt.

Study Caesar's speeches in Act IV after the death of Pothinus from the point of view of rhetoric. Why are they so effective as speeches?

Significant quotations

Each of the following quotations illustrates some aspect of the play worth your further study. Add to this list other quotations illustrative of things in the play that strike you as significant and interesting.

Alternative to the Prologue

BEL AFFRIS: They care nothing about cowardice, these Romans: they fight to win.

Act I

THE MAN: Rome is a madman's dream: this is my Reality.

I am he of whose genius you are the symbol: part brute, part woman, and part god – nothing of man in me at all. Have I read your riddle, Sphinx?

CAESAR: He will know Cleopatra by her pride, her courage, her majesty and her beauty.

Act II

CAESAR: My friend: taxes are the chief business of a conqueror of the world.

ALL THE COURTIERS: Away with you. Egypt for the Egyptians! Begone.

POTHINUS: Where is your right?

CAESAR: It is in Rufio's scabbard, Pothinus.

CAESAR: Vengeance at least is human.

THEODOTUS: What is burning there is the memory of mankind.

CAESAR: A shameful memory. Let it burn.

CAESAR: You must learn to look on battles.

Act III

CAESAR: I do not make human sacrifices to my honor, as your Druids do.

BRITANNUS: An artist! Why have they admitted this vagabond?

CAESAR (*gravely*): Cleopatra: when that trumpet sounds, we must take every man his life in his hand, and throw it in the face of Death. And of my soldiers who have trusted me there is not one whose hand I shall not hold more sacred than your head.

Act IV

FTATATEETA (*indignantly*): You are like the rest of them. You want to be what these Romans call a New Woman.

CLEOPATRA: Now that Caesar has made me wise, it is no use my liking or disliking: I do what must be done, and have no time to attend to myself.

CLEOPATRA: No, no: it is not that I am so clever, but that the others are so stupid.

POTHINUS (*musingly*): Truly, that is the great secret.

CLEOPATRA: Can one love a god? Besides, I love another Roman: one whom I saw long before Caesar—no god, but a man—one who can love and hate—one whom I can hurt and who would hurt me.

CLEOPATRA: I have not betrayed you, Caesar: I swear it.

CAESAR: I know that. I have not trusted you.

CAESAR: These knockers at your gate are also believers in vengeance and in stabbing. You have slain their leader: it is right that they shall slay you.

CAESAR (*with infinite pride*): He who has never hoped can never despair. Caesar, in good or bad fortune, looks his fate in the face.

Act V

CAESAR (*puzzled*): What do you mean by my way?

CLEOPATRA: Without punishment. Without revenge. Without judgment.

RUFIO: You are a bad hand at a bargain, mistress, if you will swop Caesar for Antony.

Find each of the above quotations in your text and decide carefully its meaning in the play.

Arrangement of material

In order to answer questions on *Caesar and Cleopatra* fully and effectively in essays you should bear in mind the following points:

(*i*) Analyse the question by dividing it into its several parts and noting all the points it implies.

(*ii*) Now try to break large questions into smaller, specific questions.

(*iii*) Note answers to your questions in brief phrases.

(*iv*) Find quotations and incidents in the text to support your points.

(*v*) Try to form a strong point of view in answer to the major question you started with.

(*vi*) Arrange your points by numbering them to make the most effective order for your arguments. Similar points may be clustered together to make up a paragraph. Check to see which are your major points, which your minor ones. Important points need more space than the others.

(*vii*) When you are satisfied with the order of your answer, write it out, giving brief quotations to support your views. Write as fluently as you can.

(*viii*) When you have finished your first version, check it carefully for errors, revising and improving it.

Specimen questions

(1) *Caesar and Cleopatra* is not a history play but a modern comedy. Do you agree?

(2) In Act IV of *Caesar and Cleopatra*, Pothinus says Cleopatra is 'a women with a Roman heart'; is this an adequate description of the change in her?

(3) Caesar is a good teacher, but Cleopatra is a poor student. From the evidence of the play, is this true?

(4) 'Caesar loves no one . . . He has no hatred in him . . .' explains Cleopatra in Act IV. From your understanding of Shaw's Caesar, how true is this assessment?

(5) Compare and contrast Shaw's portrait of Caesar with Shakespeare's in *Julius Caesar*.

(6) Compare and contrast Shaw's Cleopatra with either Shakespeare's in *Antony and Cleopatra* or Dryden's in *All for Love*.

(7) Shaw's characterisation is swift and effective, particularly in the secondary characters. Discuss his characterisation of any two of the following: Rufio, Britannus, Ftatateeta, Pothinus, Apollodorus.

(8) *Caesar and Cleopatra* has a fair amount of physical stage business. Discuss the dramatic and theatrical effect of the scuffle with the Sentinel and the business with the carpet in Act III.

(9) Discuss the language of the play, taking account of the biblical pastiche of Ra's Prologue, colloquial dialogue, the polished compliments and epigrams of Apollodorus and Caesar's rhetoric in Acts I and IV.

(10) Discuss the function of setting, sound and lighting in the play.

(11) Discuss Shaw's idea of the hero as it may be seen in *Caesar and Cleopatra*.

(12) Discuss the conflict of Rome with Egypt in *Caesar and Cleopatra* as a conflict of values.

(13) To what extent is Shaw true to his historical sources, the accounts of Caesar in Egypt found in Plutarch's *Lives* and in Theodor Mommsen's *History of Rome*?

(14) Comment on Shaw's distinction between the old and the new Rome. Is this distinction merely an effective part of Ra's Prologue speech, or has it a particular meaning within the play itself?

(15) Give examples of anachronisms in the play and explain why Shaw uses them.

Specimen answers

These are no substitute for your own interpretation of the play, nor are they the only way to answer a question: they are offered as a possible method, a guide to your own studying and writing.

(1) In note form

Caesar is a good teacher, but Cleopatra is a poor student. From the evidence of the play, is this true?

ANALYSIS OF QUESTION:

Is Caesar a teacher? Is he a good one? Is Cleopatra his student? What does he teach? What does she learn? The topic invites discussion of Caesar and Cleopatra in terms of the art of government and the Queen's change from child to adult.

BREAKDOWN INTO SMALLER QUESTIONS AND POINTS:

What lessons does Caesar teach? How does he teach? Is he strong or weak as a teacher? In what sense is Cleopatra his student? Does she want to learn? What does she learn? What does she fail to learn? Do you agree wholly, or in part, or disagree with the original question, after considering the text of the play?

BRIEF ANSWERS AND REFERENCES TO THE TEXT:

Caesar, a statesman and general, sees himself as an explorer set in a symbolic relationship to the Sphinx. Shaw reveals this in Act I, but quickly shows Caesar taking an interest in teaching Cleopatra to have courage and be like a queen by commanding her servants. Caesar also teaches Cleopatra by a trick that the Caesar she fears is only her 'old gentleman'; she can now accept him more as a friend and teacher. In Act II Caesar, although outnumbered by the Egyptians, demonstrates his own courage, humour and cleverness. His use of the bodyguard to take their leaders prisoner is effective. He also teaches mercy, based on cunning and realism. By then freeing the Egyptians to leave the palace, he has captured it without bloodshed. He also tells Cleopatra that monarchs have to work and plan their battles, as well as watching them. In Act III, Caesar's lesson is that a leader's duty to his followers comes before the interests or friendship of individuals. Acts IV and V sum up Caesar's lessons in government as follows: watch and listen; make a realistic judgment of people and situations; face facts; have courage even in the face of death; avoid mere revenge, killing not from passion but necessity only, as with the contrasting motives for the deaths of Pothinus and Ftatateeta; and improvise quickly to make the most of every situation, as when Caesar accepts Lucius Septimius and marches to meet the friendly army of Mithridates. Caesar is good at doing all this himself. He demonstrates what he teaches, but becomes impatient with Cleopatra's childishness and superstition in Act I; he fears the future of Egypt will be troublesome under her rule, and shows he is not impressed by her progress, leaving Rufio behind as governor. Cleopatra starts by being childish, superstitious and cruel as well as cowardly. Her idea of being a queen is naive in Act I: 'When I am old enough I shall do just what I like. I shall be able to poison the slaves and see them wriggle, and pretend to Ftatateeta that she is going to be put into the fiery furnace.' Her idea of Caesar and the Romans in Act I is utterly unrealistic. After her dowsing in the sea at the end of Act III and six months under Caesar's tutelage, she is well able to control her women and household. She now dominates Ftatateeta and surprises Pothinus so much by her adult behaviour and new confidence that he admits she has changed. Quote her speech beginning, 'When I was foolish, I did what I liked, except when Ftatateeta beat me' (Act IV). She has shed her adolescent conceit, which we saw in the first two acts. She now has insight into herself, Pothinus and Caesar. She is politically realistic when she replies to Pothinus's 'Is Cleopatra then indeed a Queen, and no longer Caesar's prisoner and slave?' with her best insight, 'Pothinus: we are all Caesar's slaves—all we in this land of Egypt—whether we will or not. And she who is wise enough to know this will reign when Caesar departs.' She realises Caesar does not love her. She demonstrates her new strength and her use of Caesar's friendship so effectively that Pothinus angrily refers to her as 'a woman with a Roman heart' and threatens that 'Whilst I live, she shall never rule.' From Cleopatra's point of view, Pothinus's death is a necessity: from Caesar's, it is rash and dangerous to murder him. Cleopatra has learned a great deal very quickly. She has grown to be regal and womanly. Her passion can be satisfied only by Antony. Rufio in Act V sees her preference for Antony over Caesar as foolish; Caesar, however, is no lover. Shaw enables us to see Cleopatra as an apt student of Caesar, marred by her need for bloodshed and passion. By the end of the play, though, she has gained more than she has lost.

MAIN THESIS:

On the whole Caesar is a good teacher, but Cleopatra, though imperfect, is a quick and responsive student after losing her conceitedness.

FIRST VERSION:

Arrange the points made above in the order you find to be best. Paragraph divisions may suggest themselves. Check the text for other quotations to support your points. Cut anything which seems irrelevant or too trivial. Write out your essay on one side of your sheets of paper only. This will give you space for alterations.

Make any necessary cuts, additions or alterations to your first version. You may now rewrite the piece as your final version.

(2) In essay form

(a) Caesar and Cleopatra has a fair amount of physical stage business. Discuss the dramatic and theatrical effect of the scuffle with the Sentinel and the business with the carpet.

The physical stage business of Act III of *Caesar and Cleopatra* contrasts with the lengthy dialogues of the first two acts. This shift in focus allows the audience to relax, absorbing what has happened so far, and enjoy some broad comedy. Some of this comedy arises from the scuffle with the Sentinel and the carpet business.

The scuffle has two parts. In the first, Apollodorus is dashing and gallant as well as quick-witted, artistic and witty. This manner and his disregard of the Sentinel's orders rather than his aestheticism provoke the soldier. Shaw uses the encounter to contrast these aspects of Apollodorus with the stolid and slow-witted sentry, who doggedly follows orders yet ultimately fails in his duty to keep Cleopatra in the palace. The encounter also serves to reinforce our view of Ftatateeta as a strong and deadly old woman. Her grabbing the soldier from behind in a bear-like grip adds to the comedy, but also prepares us to accept the fact that she would be capable of killing Pothinus in Act IV. The contrast between Apollodorus and Ftatateeta is further brought out in this episode by his mercy, when he refuses to kill the soldier, and the old nurse's callousness when she cries, 'Thrust your knife into the dog's throat.' The contrast in their physical appearance and character adds to the comedy, and makes the Centurion's notion that the pair might be married very funny.

Theatrically, the first little scuffle gives us some excitement at the prospect of a fight on stage. The tension mounts as the Sentinel threatens to spear Apollodorus, but this quickly changes to farce as the old nurse pinions the soldier's arms. The second encounter between Apollodorus and the Sentinel is more spectacular: the Sentinel hurls his pilum, and Apollodorus expertly ducks to avoid a hit. Meanwhile, the boatman adds a comic touch to the proceedings by peeping cautiously over the quayside to watch the fight. The swordplay is made comic by the soldier's constant fear that the old nurse will get him.

Dramatically, Shaw uses this second encounter to further the characterisation of Apollodorus by revealing his loyalty to Cleopatra and his eye to gaining her business. Both encounters, of course, show a Roman soldier as an ordinary, rather surly man (a good minor role for a comic actor) rather than a formidable, invincible warrior.

The business with the carpets also falls into two main parts outside the palace, but it reaches its climax at the lighthouse. Theatrically, the four porters carrying rolls of carpet afford much opportunity for comedy when they go past the preoccupied sentinel and later, when they appear handling their load in a gingerly way to avoid harming Cleopatra, who is concealed inside. In the hands of good actors, the loading of the little boat could make a humorous episode. Cleopatra's exchange with Apollodorus would gain point from the comic business of almost dropping the carpet:

FTATATEETA *(anxiously)*: In the name of the gods, Apollodorus, run no risks with that bale.

APOLLODORUS: Fear not, thou venerable grotesque.

The arrival of the carpet at the lighthouse is theatrically spectacular, for it involves the use of the crane to haul it from the boat. Apollodorus *'is swinging in the air with his bale of carpet at the end of it'*. His athletic action, song and high-spirits add to the fun of the episode.

The dramatic functions of the carpet business are varied. Firstly, the goods themselves help to establish our image of Apollodorus as a dealer in costly and beautiful things. Secondly, a new aspect of Cleopatra is shown to us: she is ingenious and persistent in her determination to join Caesar against his wishes. The fears expressed that Cleopatra will be dropped into the sea during the carpet business serve thirdly to prepare us for the climax of the entire act, when Cleopatra is, after so much careful handling, unceremoniously thrown into the sea. Finally, the mood of fun and comic plotting, which reaches its resolution when Cleopatra is pulled out of the carpet, make a strong contrast to Caesar's brushing her aside to follow the course of the battle. The switch in mood from laughter to grimness and Cleopatra's tears is a powerful effect, preparing for the change in Cleopatra we find in Act IV.

In some performances of the play, Act III was cut. From the point of view of plot, this would not matter much, but the comic business gives much enjoyment, introduces a lively new character in Apollodorus and leads eventually to the harsh lesson Cleopatra learns on the fringe of the action of opposing armies: that she is not indispensable.

(B) Discuss Shaw's idea of the hero as it may be seen in Caesar and Cleopatra.

In *Caesar and Cleopatra,* Shaw presents several images of the hero. Cleopatra's idea of the hero is that he is a lover: strong, handsome and powerful. This type is, of course, Antony, but though he is mentioned, Shaw keeps him deliberately out of the play. Bel Affris is a young nobleman of the Queen's guards. In An Alternative to the Prologue he appears *'battlestained; and his left forearm, bandaged, comes through a torn sleeve.*' He is a hero common in drama: a valiant young soldier. But Shaw also calls him 'a fairhaired dandy'; this makes him comparable in some ways to Apollodorus, who is young, brave and a fashionable aesthete, loving fine clothes and costly goods. But Apollodorus is not so much a military hero, as a type, the amateur swordsman who fights to serve his friends or a lady. These two characters make a pair, illustrating types of hero common in the theatre and played by the juvenile lead. Yet in Shaw's play, both these types are deliberately given minor roles.

Shaw embodies a different idea of the hero in Caesar, his main character. The three conventional types of hero (the lover, the swashbuckling officer and the dashing duellist) Shaw uses as foils against which Caesar stands out in sharp contrast. Caesar is not a lover in Shaw's play. His relationship to Cleopatra is more that of a mentor and an uncle. He is not young and handsome but middle-aged, long-nosed and bald. At the end of Act II Cleopatra wounds his vanity by making fun of his baldness.

Caesar's character and exploits are, by ordinary standards, as unheroic as his appearance. Although in Act I, Cleopatra fears the fierce and bloodthirsty monster which is the Caesar of her imagination, the real Caesar turns out to be her 'old gentleman' who actually teaches her to behave as if she is unafraid. In Act II, Caesar's first thought when he meets the Egyptian leaders belongs not to the conventional hero, but to the market-place: 'Now, Pothinus, to business. I am badly in want of money.'

Shaw's Caesar is no intrepid swordsman. When in danger, he calls his bodyguard in Act II. Nor is he always right, for the battle on the waterfront in Act III shows that Caesar has miscalculated. The Egyptians cut him off from his men, who are now trapped on the mole, and Caesar is forced to escape by an undignified jump into the sea. In fact, Shaw presents Caesar's military exploits in Egypt not as an heroic struggle with a small force of Romans against a much larger Egyptian army, but as a series of hastily improvised tricks and stratagems. Caesar is ultimately victorious only because of the arrival of his ally, Mithridates, with an army. Rufio, the practical military man, is annoyed by Caesar's use of cunning. In Act II, when Caesar explains that he has freed his prisoners so that soldiers are not wasted as guards, Rufio replies: 'Agh! I might have known there was some fox's trick behind your fine talking.' And when Caesar explains that he has manipulated Theodotus into using the Egyptian army to put out the library fire rather than defend the lighthouse, Rufio, disgusted with Caesar, exclaims at the end of Act II, 'More foxing! Agh!'

If Shaw's Caesar is not a hero of the usual kind, he nevertheless has some admirable qualities. He is not merely an anti-hero with nothing to recommend him as a model of behaviour. Shaw makes it clear that although Caesar is a statesman rather than an heroic general, some of his qualities make him outstanding and greater than other men. In Act IV Shaw stresses his hero's realistic attitudes to life. Caesar does not waste time resenting inevitabilities, such as Cleopatra's treachery, or her preference for Antony; 'Shall I resent youth when it turns from age, and ambition when it turns from servitude?' In this act, Caesar's calm, diplomacy, and imagination come to the fore. He sees how empires may fall, and sees the need for new centres of civilisation. He asks Cleopatra:

> 'Shall we leave Rome behind us – Rome, that has achieved greatness only to learn how greatness destroys nations of men who are not great! Shall I make you a new kingdom, and build you a holy city there in the great unknown?'

But as Caesar's imagination soars, so that he is like the romantic figure who confronted the Sphinx in Act I, and Cleopatra rapturously responds, Rufio is grumbling and Ftatateeta is already preparing to kill Pothinus. In this act Shaw contrasts the best sides of Caesar with a changed Cleopatra, who can yet cry out for blood. Caesar's great speech against vengeance is the rhetoric of an unheroic man who seeks the arts of good government and peace rather than murder.

Cleopatra in Act V sums up Caesar's way of ruling as 'Without punishment. Without revenge. Without judgment.' Caesar calls it 'the right way, the great way, the only possible way in the end.' For him, and for Shaw in this play, the true hero is the statesman who governs in this manner, bringing peace.

Part 5

Suggestions for further reading

The text

The official text of the play is in the volume *Three Plays for Puritans* in *The Standard Edition of the Works of Bernard Shaw*, Constable, London, 1931–1950, 36 volumes. This is the best and fullest edition of Shaw's works.

SHAW, BERNARD: *Three Plays for Puritans*, Penguin Books, Harmondsworth, 1954. This is a paperback version of the same volume in the Constable Standard Edition. It is readily available and contains Shaw's Preface, his notes and two other plays: *The Devil's Disciple* and *Captain Brassbound's Conversion*. It is therefore the handiest edition to use and is the one on which these notes are based.

SHAW, BERNARD: *Caesar and Cleopatra*, Longmans Green, London, 1963, with an introduction and notes by A. C. Ward. This is the best annotated edition of the play.

General reading

BROWN, IVOR: *Shaw in his Time*, Nelson, London, 1965. This is the best short background study to appear recently. It has a useful chronology of Shaw's life.

CHESTERTON, G. K.: *Bernard Shaw*, Bodley Head, London, 1909, 1935; Hill and Wang, New York, 1956. This is still very pleasurable and provocative reading.

COLBOURNE, MAURICE: *The Real Bernard Shaw*, Dent, London, 1949. This is useful for giving an actor's view of the playwright. It contains a chronology of Shaw's life and of productions of his plays.

Biography

ERVINE, ST. JOHN: *Bernard Shaw, His Life, Work, and Friends*, William Morrow, New York, 1956. A large biography, this is less reliable than Henderson, but more readable.

HENDERSON, ARCHIBALD: *George Bernard Shaw: Man of the Century*, Appleton-Century-Crofts, New York, 1956. The third of Henderson's biographies of Shaw, it incorporates material from the earlier ones.

PEARSON, HESKETH: *G. B. S. A Full Length Portrait and a Postscript,* Harper and Brothers, New York, 1942; 1950. Published in England as *Bernard Shaw: His Life And Personality,* Collins, London, 1942. This study is racy and very readable.

Background history

YOUNG, G. M.: *Victorian England: Portrait of an Age,* Oxford University Press, London, 1960. An excellent social history for background reading.

Critical books

BENTLEY, ERIC: *Bernard Shaw, 1856–1950,* New Directions, New York, 1957. Valuable dramatic criticism.

CARPENTER, C. A.: *Bernard Shaw and the Art of Destroying Ideals: The Early Plays,* University of Wisconsin Press, Madison, 1969. This deals with Shaw as a moral iconoclast.

CROMPTON, LOUIS: *Shaw the Dramatist,* University of Nebraska Press, Lincoln, 1969. A sound study of social, historical and philosophical backgrounds to twelve major plays.

MACCARTHY, SIR DESMOND: *Shaw: the Plays,* David and Charles, Newton Abbot, 1973. This is a useful collection of MacCarthy's theatre reviews of Shaw's plays.

MEISEL, MARTIN: *Shaw and the Nineteenth Century Theatre,* Princeton University Press, Princeton, 1963. Puts Shaw in context.

WISENTHAL, J. L.: *The Marriage of Contraries. Bernard Shaw's Middle Plays,* Harvard University Press, Cambridge, Massachusetts, 1974. This book deals with plays written later than *Three Plays for Puritans,* but it usefully discusses Shaw's habit of seeing things in terms of conflicts and contraries.

The author of these notes

ANDREW PARKIN, who is a graduate of the Universities of Cambridge and Bristol, teaches English at the University of British Columbia, Canada. He has also taught in England and Hong Kong.

He is editor of *The Canadian Journal of Irish Studies,* and has published many book reviews and articles. Editor of *Stage One: A Canadian Scenebook,* Toronto, 1973, he is interested in the staging and performance of plays. He has worked, too, on modern Arab plays as English reviser for M. A. Manzalaoui's collection, *Arab Writing Today, 2: Drama,* Cairo, 1977.

Andrew Parkin's most recent publication is his critical book, *The Dramatic Imagination of W. B. Yeats,* Dublin, 1978.

YORK NOTES

The first 100 titles

CHINUA ACHEBE	*Arrow of God* *Things Fall Apart*
JANE AUSTEN	*Northanger Abbey* *Pride and Prejudice* *Sense and Sensibility*
ROBERT BOLT	*A Man For All Seasons*
CHARLOTTE BRONTË	*Jane Eyre*
EMILY BRONTË	*Wuthering Heights*
ALBERT CAMUS	*L'Etranger (The Outsider)*
GEOFFREY CHAUCER	*Prologue to the Canterbury Tales* *The Franklin's Tale* *The Knight's Tale* *The Nun's Priest's Tale* *The Pardoner's Tale*
SIR ARTHUR CONAN DOYLE	*The Hound of the Baskervilles*
JOSEPH CONRAD	*Nostromo*
DANIEL DEFOE	*Robinson Crusoe*
CHARLES DICKENS	*David Copperfield* *Great Expectations*
GEORGE ELIOT	*Adam Bede* *Silas Marner* *The Mill on the Floss*
T. S. ELIOT	*The Waste Land*
WILLIAM FAULKNER	*As I Lay Dying*
F. SCOTT FITZGERALD	*The Great Gatsby*
E. M. FORSTER	*A Passage to India*
ATHOL FUGARD	*Selected Plays*
MRS GASKELL	*North and South*
WILLIAM GOLDING	*Lord of the Flies*

OLIVER GOLDSMITH	*The Vicar of Wakefield*
THOMAS HARDY	*Jude the Obscure* *Tess of the D'Urbervilles* *The Mayor of Casterbridge* *The Return of the Native* *The Trumpet Major*
L. P. HARTLEY	*The Go-Between*
ERNEST HEMINGWAY	*For Whom the Bell Tolls* *The Old Man and the Sea*
ANTHONY HOPE	*The Prisoner of Zenda*
RICHARD HUGHES	*A High Wind in Jamaica*
THOMAS HUGHES	*Tom Brown's Schooldays*
HENRIK IBSEN	*A Doll's House*
HENRY JAMES	*The Turn of the Screw*
BEN JONSON	*The Alchemist* *Volpone*
D. H. LAWRENCE	*Sons and Lovers* *The Rainbow*
HARPER LEE	*To Kill a Mocking-Bird*
SOMERSET MAUGHAM	*Selected Short Stories*
HERMAN MELVILLE	*Billy Budd* *Moby Dick*
ARTHUR MILLER	*Death of a Salesman* *The Crucible*
JOHN MILTON	*Paradise Lost I & II*
SEAN O'CASEY	*Juno and the Paycock*
GEORGE ORWELL	*Animal Farm* *Nineteen Eighty-four*
JOHN OSBORNE	*Look Back in Anger*
HAROLD PINTER	*The Birthday Party*
J. D. SALINGER	*The Catcher in the Rye*
SIR WALTER SCOTT	*Ivanhoe* *Quentin Durward*

WILLIAM SHAKESPEARE	*A Midsummer Night's Dream*
	Antony and Cleopatra
	Coriolanus
	Cymbeline
	Hamlet
	Henry IV Part I
	Henry V
	Julius Caesar
	King Lear
	Macbeth
	Measure for Measure
	Othello
	Richard II
	Romeo and Juliet
	The Merchant of Venice
	The Tempest
	The Winter's Tale
	Troilus and Cressida
	Twelfth Night
GEORGE BERNARD SHAW	*Androcles and the Lion*
	Arms and the Man
	Caesar and Cleopatra
	Pygmalion
RICHARD BRINSLEY SHERIDAN	*The School for Scandal*
JOHN STEINBECK	*Of Mice and Men*
	The Grapes of Wrath
	The Pearl
ROBERT LOUIS STEVENSON	*Kidnapped*
	Treasure Island
JONATHAN SWIFT	*Gulliver's Travels*
W. M. THACKERAY	*Vanity Fair*
MARK TWAIN	*Huckleberry Finn*
	Tom Sawyer
VOLTAIRE	*Candide*
H. G. WELLS	*The History of Mr Polly*
	The Invisible Man
	The War of the Worlds
OSCAR WILDE	*The Importance of Being Earnest*